Natural Selling Concepts

THE BEST WAY TO SELL

Carl Bromer

B-ELITE PUBLISHING

DAYTON, OHIO

Second Printing 2005
Published by:
B-Elite Publishing, Inc.
P.O.Box 751705
Dayton, Ohio 45475-1705
(937) 291-0340
Fax (937) 291-2113
Website: www.B-Elite.com
Contact author: carlb@B-Elite.com
Contact for orders: joshb@B-Elite.com
Contact for speakers: info@B-Elite.com

ISBN 0-9745736-0-4 (hardcover)
ISBN 0-9745736-1-2 (paperback)

Library of Congress Control Number: 2003098097

Book design: Janice M. Phelps
Special thanks to Karen Saunders for help with illustrations.
PRINTED IN THE UNITED STATES OF AMERICA

Bulk discounts are available to businesses and other organizations.
Please contact (937) 291-0340.

Dedicated to Pamela Bromer,
my wife, my love, my best friend, and
the best person I will ever know this side of heaven.

Acknowledgments

First, I would like to acknowledge that the concepts and principles used in this book are timeless. Four thousand years ago, Solomon wrote, *"What has been will be again, what has been done will be done again; there is nothing new under the sun. Is there anything of which one can say, 'Look! This is something new'? It was here already, long ago; it was here before our time."* None of the principles used in this book are new. However, their application to selling throughout this book will be very new to the vast majority of readers.

I would like to acknowledge some of the many people who have played significant roles in helping me to apply these concepts and principles to the selling profession.

First, my mother, Winnie Bromer Vickers and my wife, Pamela. They have always believed in me, even when there was no evidence to support their beliefs. To them I am eternally grateful.

I am also indebted to my brother Tom Bromer, who has been a constant source of encouragement . . . first, to start the book . . . then to complete it and see it through to publication. I can honestly say this book would not have been completed without his gentle and uplifting prodding. He made me feel like a successful author before I even started writing.

Two mentors helped mold my business ethics and values. Jim Schindler, who exemplified integrity and love in a way that only a father or older brother could do, has been my business and personal growth mentor. Jim is more than a mentor; he's a true friend. Roy Linton, who served as CEO for Standard Register during some of their most successful years, and who recently went to be with his eternal Father in heaven, was my sales mentor. Roy reeked with common sense. He had a way of taking the most complicated selling and business situation and blowing away the smoke to make it look simple. Roy was also more than a mentor. He was an inspiration and a genuinely good man.

Jim Kill and Nina Fickes are the two best coworkers a person could ever have. Jim and Nina have played critical parts in the development and publication of this book. Jim has worked with me for years to test and refine the principles we teach, and Nina has worked tirelessly on original manuscripts that were hardly legible, much less publishable. I am deeply indebted to them both.

A number of students at Cedarville University helped in the early editing stages and I want to recognize each. They made a significant contribution to the development of the principles and concepts that are covered in this book. They are: Kevin Batista, Adrianne Bozick, Susan Brownlee, Thomas Burleigh, Stephanie Candler, Amber Durbin, Cheryl Elliott, Michael Freeze, Glori Goheen, Sara Kilgore, Amy Gregory, Kathleen McGunnigal, Kara Moore, Casey Schmidt, Kerri Sheldon, Brady Spitzer, and Joel Tomkinson.

Some of the sharpest business people in the world have helped me to test the concepts and techniques that are now the foundation of this book. It would not be possible to name them all. I do want to recognize and thank those who had a significant ongoing influence on my development and on the testing of the material in this book. They are: Pete Gorka, Mike Salvatore, Dale Ainsworth, Steve Walters, Doug Griffith, Jim Gross, Brent Nichols, Frank Sanders, Bill Sanders, Steve Blackburn, Jerry Perrich, Mark Jacobson, Jim Jacobson, Lee Murray, Don Moxley, Larry Curk, Bob Phillips, Lee Wagoner, Dave McDine, George Petzelt, Jeff Rex, Susan Chicoine, Lynn Trainor, Ron

Acknowledgments

Braswell, Bruce Carter, Mike Gerace, Jim Hollander, Warren Herminghausen, Don Carone, Bob Jahn, Maureen Patterson, Bud Ragan, Mike Hamilton, Michael Propst, Bob Walker, Mitch Rhodus, John Bunn, Fred Booher, Karl Fetzer, George Kuykendall, Kim Nierman, Jay Schindler, Mike Schindler, Mark Schindler, and Dave Schindler.

Josh Bromer (my son) and Karen Saunders helped in the design of many of the illustrations. Their positive and creative contributions are evident throughout the book.

I want to especially thank Janice Phelps who edited this into a real book. She designed and polished and worked her magic to the point where some people now believe I can write. She has made me look good and she has made this a better book.

Prior to giving this book to Janice for her final editing, I asked a number of very sharp business associates who were already familiar with *Natural Selling Concepts* to read the manuscript and make suggestions. These people each had a major positive impact on the first draft. Each is a personal friend and each has my eternal gratitude and respect. They are: Steve Chaisson, Steve Compton, Harold Daniel, Lowell Dye, Don Harris and Harold Varvel.

Finally, I would be nothing were it not for the people who have helped mold me into the person I am. Like it or not, they must accept part of the responsibility. I love each one and thank God for placing them in my life. In addition to my family already mentioned, I would like to thank my brothers Bill and Mike, my sons Chris, Mark and Jeff with his wife Beth and their children — Keaton, Morgan and Kylie; also, Nancy, Jonathan, Katherine, Kim, Daniel, Gisela, Georg, Ginny, Kevin and Bill Vickers. They have each encouraged me in special ways and I am eternally grateful for all of them.

Table of Contents

Figures

Preface

Why I Decided to Write this Book

Thirty-two years ago, I started selling. Fresh out of college with an electrical engineering degree, I wanted to go into business, but I wasn't sure which avenue to take. I assumed that selling would be a good foundation for any future effort so I began working as a telephone salesperson for an electronic components distributor in Dayton, Ohio. My first few weeks were busy, but not productive. I sold nothing.

I received no training, knew little about the distribution business and even less about selling. But there I was, and actually I enjoyed it. The work was fast-paced, and once I learned the procedure for checking stock and writing orders, I began to feel competent. Then, Uncle Sam decided I needed to spend time in the military, so I joined the U.S. Air Force and spent the next five years as a pilot.

Returning to civilian life, I first went to work for a small company selling electronic components, and I eventually moved on to the consumer products division of Texas Instruments.

In all this time, the only sales training I received came from books I took the initiative to read. None of the companies I worked for provided sales training. Texas Instruments had an awesome product-knowledge training program, and I did learn a lot about consumer products . . . but nothing on sales technique.

I started attending motivational talks by Zig Ziglar, Art Linkletter, Herb True, and others, and I loved it! Their presentations included motivational stories about average people who had achieved phenomenal sales success. They said I could achieve great results, too. All I had to do was work hard and have a good attitude. For the first time, I actually felt that I was learning what it took to sell and succeed in the real world. My sales started going up, and I felt I was on my way.

However, a funny thing happened on the way to phenomenal success. I hit a brick wall — in fact I hit many brick walls. Every time I attended a seminar or read a motivational book, I would be energized for a few weeks, and then it would wear off. Smack! Right into another brick wall! I couldn't figure out what was wrong until I read a book on "strategic selling," and it hit me that there were other types of sales training.

I had been exposed to product-knowledge training by my employer and motivational training through speakers and books, but now I learned there was strategic sales training as well. Strategic selling differs in that it focuses on strategy and planning: the things you should do *before* you call on a prospect.

It took me another two years of roller-coaster results to realize that strategic selling didn't provide all the answers either. While it seemed as if the sales trainers teaching product knowledge were not working salespeople themselves, and the motivational sales trainers selling books and tapes didn't seem to live in the same world that I lived in, strategic trainers were even worse! They philosophized about the right way to sell, though they themselves hardly ever left the safety of their academic cocoons.

These trainers (most, not all) had long ago forgotten what it was like to have a real person say, *"I want to think it over . . . Your prices are ridiculous . . . My current supplier is a great friend . . . I had a bad experience with your company before they hired you . . . I have to get twelve competitive bids"* . . . *and on and on . . .*

Preface

These trainers were not teaching how to sell in the real world . . . some never did! Now I don't mean to sound negative on the whole "training scene." Just most of it! Some, like Zig Ziglar, have had a profound and positive impact on my career and personal life. In fact, I listened to Zig Ziglar's tapes so many times when I was starting out that I started speaking with a Mississippi accent. There are other men and women who do a fantastic job teaching people how to sell, but a significant number of people in sales training are actually unemployed salespeople, currently between jobs and using the title "Consultant" or "Coach."

Armed with what I had discovered working in the real world of sales, I developed my own sales training program. I offered it to other salespeople who I knew and it really took off, eventually becoming a full-time business. Two years later, in the late Seventies, Ira Hayes attended my program. Mr. Hayes was a motivational speaker on the national speaking circuit and was known all over the world as "Mr. Enthusiasm." I had called him and pestered him until he agreed to be my guest. I figured if he liked my program, he might even endorse it.

Afterward Mr. Hayes commented, "You've got a pretty okay program here, but you need to be careful."

That wasn't exactly the ringing endorsement I was looking for — and what did he mean, I need to be careful?

"If you're not careful," he continued, "you too will soon be teaching pleasantries and platitudes, and if you stay out of real selling long enough, you will become jaded and start teaching things that sound good but don't work."

After I recovered from the shock of his evaluation, I decided to research the experiences of my past clients, and, to my horror, I found that I was like most of the other sales trainers, and my clients were facing the same real-world challenges that I had years earlier. They liked my program and commented positively on it, but they couldn't attribute any real-world sales to my teaching. In fact, many of them remembered having a good time but couldn't remember a single thing of significance from the program. I was forced to admit I was teaching things that sounded good but didn't work. I was devastated.

In fact, I decided to shut down my training business. I could not, in good conscience, sell a program that I didn't believe in. I could not look someone in the eye and promise, "This program will help you to get better results."

I returned to business-to-business selling and committed myself to carefully studying what really did work. The process took ten years, but it was worth it.

The company that became my laboratory was Eskco, Inc. in Dayton, Ohio. Eventually, I re-wrote my sales training program to reflect the real-world things I had learned. This new program took off and was eventually offered through the Dayton Chamber of Commerce. Salespeople started calling to tell me about customers and new orders they were receiving as a direct result of the program. That program was the great-grandfather of this book.

Working at Eskco was enjoyable, and the people were like family to me. It was such a great place to work and grow that I stayed on an extra five years for a total of fifteen years and might have never left had the sales training business not grown to demand so much of my time.

Yet there remained one problem that needed to be solved. How could I go back to full-time training and not become jaded and ineffective as Ira Hayes had warned? The answer was right in front of me.

Instead of just telling people how to sell, I would offer to go and do it with them and for them. Using this process, the program evolved into *Natural Selling Concepts*. I called it *Natural* because it taught principles and techniques that did not require people to change from their natural style into some slick, obnoxious, cartoon-style character that many salespeople seem to become.

I started by offering the program to members of several large chambers of commerce. The chambers endorsed the program, thousands of their members attended and I regularly made real sales calls with some of the members.

By offering the *Natural Selling Concepts* program, the chambers provided a valuable service to their members — especially smaller companies that could not afford to bring a major program in-house. *Natural Selling Concepts* received recognition as a real-world sales training program that taught salespeople how to get practical, measurable results.

Soon, I started receiving requests to provide in-house training for some of the larger companies who had sent people to our chamber of commerce programs.

After a few years of working on my own, Jim Kill (a world-class speaker and sales-trainer) from Griffin, Georgia, joined me. To this day, we continue to make sales calls with real salespeople, and the *Natural Selling Concepts* seminar has subsequently developed into one of the most effective and highly rated training programs in the world.

So, there you have it.

This book is the result of years of observation, aggravation, participation and celebration. We watch, we study, we participate. We get frustrated when customers do not behave rationally . . . and we celebrate our victories when it all comes together.

There's nothing quite like having an alumnus call and tell us about the big prospects who aren't getting away. In fact, it's not unusual for people in two-day programs to close difficult orders during their lunch hour on the second day of the program. And, we have testimonials from people who attended our program ten years ago who are still using the techniques learned in *Natural Selling Concepts.*

This book will guide you through the *Natural Selling Process* and show you ways to identify, qualify and close on more business deals than you might have dreamed possible.

If you are new to selling, my goal is that you will say, "Gee, that's easy! I don't have to be rude, crude and obnoxious to be successful in sales. I can be myself. I can be a natural salesperson, and I can win!"

If you have been selling for thirty years or more, my goal is that you will say, "It sure would have been a lot easier if I had been doing this when I first started. I hesitate to think how much further I would have been by now."

You be the judge. Apply the principles and techniques in this book and your ability to sell will accelerate. If you don't try, I personally guarantee they will not work! If you do sincerely try, I personally guarantee that they will work. The choice is yours.

Introduction

During the early 1980s, the Japanese captured the high-profit portion of the American automobile business.

How did they do it?

In the 1960s, "Made in Japan" meant trinkets and trash or worse yet, poorly manufactured junk. However, in a very short period of time, the Japanese had more than achieved world-class quality. They redefined quality, and the rest is history. It took America over fifteen years to catch up, and some manufacturers are still behind.

Japan's process of redefining quality actually started when an American, Dr. W. Edwards Deming, went to Japan where he taught the use of statistics to measure and manage quality.

Deming's theory was simple. If you could break the automobile down into its component parts, and then make one part at least 1% better by improving the manufacturing process, then you would have a better automobile. Perform the process on each part and go for more than 1% improvement and eventually you would have the best.

By definition, there's only one "best." But best today may not be best tomorrow. Best is not static. Since there's no upper limit on quality, theoretically there's no upper limit on the best.

How does this relate to selling?

Well, if you break the selling process down into its component parts and then learn how to do each part a little better and continue to perfect each part, then you will *become your best at selling.*

Natural Selling Concepts

That's what *Natural Selling Concepts* is designed to do. It's designed to help you to become your best and stay your best whether you are new to sales or have years of sales experience.

I want you to be your best. Being your best means you will go beyond your current best. Maybe even all the way to redefining sales quality like the Japanese redefined manufacturing quality in the 1980s.

By the way, while the Japanese were redefining quality in the automobile industry in America, they were also redefining quality in the watch industry in Switzerland and the camera industry in Germany.

How do you become YOUR best?

I encourage you to read this book as though I wrote it to you personally.

If you are new to sales, this book will tell you how to succeed in selling. Mastering *Natural Selling Concepts* will accelerate your success.

If you have been selling for many years, *it is even more critical* that you master *Natural Selling Concepts*. Many of the techniques and practices in *Natural Selling Concepts* are new and unique. Please do not assume that you already know "how to sell." Assuming will cause you to miss growth opportunities in the form of principles and techniques that could make a significant impact on your results.

What are the goals for *Natural Selling Concepts*?

I have two major goals. First, to cause you to change . . . for the better . . . so you can get better results . . . forever! Change sounds easy, but it's uncomfortable! That's why so few people do it!

My second goal is to show you how to plan and execute world-class sales calls in the real world with people who sometimes say, "No!" We will do this by looking at the parts of a sales call and seeing how you can do each part the best.

Are YOU qualified?

Some people will achieve phenomenal success as a result of applying the principles from this book . . . but not everyone. You can and you will, but first:

- You must be willing to grow . . . you must be willing to change.
- You must be willing to learn new techniques.
- You must be willing to try new techniques even if you disagree or are uncomfortable or stumble at first.
- You must have a desire to be your best and the commitment to do the work to become your best.

Olympic and professional ice-skaters know the difference between a double Lutz and a double Axel. Most of the rest of us do not. We could learn the difference in less than fifteen minutes if they showed us a slow motion, side-by-side video with the take-off, mid-air turns and landing. However, would you agree that it would probably take a bit longer than fifteen minutes to learn how to execute one?

All new things are difficult at first! At one point in your life, washing your hands and face and changing your pants were impossible, but you worked your way through that. The same is true with selling. You can work your way through to becoming your best at selling too.

Are you qualified? You must be or you wouldn't still be reading this!

A word of caution!

Go through this material with an open mind. The principles are universal.

Don't get hung up on titles or specific examples that might not relate to your industry. Look for the principles!

Natural Selling Concepts

All through this book I will use the word "prospect" to mean anyone who makes a decision that you are trying to influence. It might be a company owner, a purchasing agent, a human resources executive, an engineer, a stock clerk or any other title. It might even be your children or your spouse. Basically, it's anyone you are trying to influence to make a decision. It's anyone you are trying to sell.

Don't jump forward or assume you will not need a particular chapter or section. Each part of this book has critical information you will need to know.

Starting Point . . . Define "Selling"

Have you ever wondered how salespeople got such a poor reputation? You know it's true. In fact, we even have proof that most folks do not like salespeople.

Proof #1: Webster's dictionary gives a fairly comprehensive definition of "sell." Check it out. You will find that the word "sell" has more than fifteen different uses and most of them are negative. Words like cheat, dupe, hoax, and take advantage are typical. (Typical definitions are shown at the end of this chapter.)

For the balance of this book, I will refer to "Webster selling" as the kind of rude, crude and obnoxious selling that none of us like, but so many untrained salespeople do.

Proof #2: Selling is one of the most critical disciplines for any organization. Most CEOs of large successful organizations have direct selling experience. Profit and non-profit organizations depend on their ability to "sell" benefits to customers, supporters, employees, stockholders, suppliers, etc. Yet, of more than twenty-five thousand institutions of higher learning in the United States (colleges and universities), none offer a bachelor's or master's degree in "Selling."

Introduction

Few people grow up in America wanting to become salespeople. That's why colleges don't offer majors in it. Colleges know that if they did offer majors in selling, nobody would come.

Proof #3: The Saturn Automobile Company spent millions of dollars advertising in the 1990s, telling people, "If you come to our dealership, you will not have to deal with incentivized salespeople." Why would they advertise that way if the public liked salespeople?

It's sad but true that most people do not like salespeople.

Why?

Ineffective and time-wasting salespeople are everywhere. If "Webster selling" were against the law, many salespeople would even be in jail.

So, if Webster defines what selling *is,* how do we define what selling *should* be?

One definition that I heard years ago said, "Selling is providing goods and services that *don't* come back to customers who *do* come back." Another said, "Selling is getting someone to make a decision or take an action that they might not make or do if you were not there influencing them." Both of these definitions are accurate. However, they both allow room for the Webster kind of selling mentioned earlier.

The definition we developed for *Natural Selling Concepts* is as follows:

Selling is finding people who have needs that your products and services can satisfy and then filling those needs in such a way that you and your customer both make a profit or gain.

Natural Selling Concepts

If your customer doesn't make a gain, you are a "Webster salesperson." If you don't make a gain, you are on your way out of business.

Also, our definition has two of the most significant parts of your job description as a salesperson.

1. Finding people . . . prospecting and developing relationships, and;

2. Filling needs . . . closing . . . precipitating action . . . getting your prospect to make a decision and then act on it!

Finding people and filling needs, along with all of the other disciplines necessary to be successful in selling, will be covered in subsequent chapters of this book.

What else do you need to consider before you get started?

Natural Selling Concepts is dedicated to the proposition that all salespeople have a natural style. It's a combination of personality and values. Some people are aggressive, some are passive, some are extroverted and some are introverted. No matter what your current style is, you do not have to change your personality or lower your values to become a top-notch salesperson. You can become great with your current natural style if you will just follow some basic concepts.

This book identifies thirty *Natural Selling Concepts* that are based on timeless principles. I firmly believe there are no "secrets" to success in selling, only basic concepts that drive success, and they are not new.

Natural Selling Concepts is based on these concepts that do not change. Techniques and styles change; *Natural Selling Concepts* do not. You will do your best if you understand and apply these concepts to your selling career.

NATURAL SELLING CONCEPT #1

The key to success has always been in the basics. The basics that guide sales success do not change, and they are not a secret.

Whenever someone does something outstanding or achieves great success, the world beats a path to their door to ask them, "What's your secret?"

It must be a secret or everyone would have done it! Right? Well, Casey Stengel was one of the most successful managers in baseball history. He led the New York Yankees to ten World Series (1949-1953, 1955-1958, and 1960); and seven World Series championships (1949-1953, 1956, and 1958), including a record of five consecutive titles (1949-1953). What was Casey Stengel's "secret?"

Casey Stengel had no secret! He understood that real success was determined by the basics. In baseball, the basics are run, hit, throw, catch and slide. Casey knew that all teams had great players. They wouldn't be in the pros if they weren't great. But he also knew that games were always won and lost on the fundamentals — the basics!

Watch the next World Series! Both teams will make great plays, but the team that wins will be the one that best executes the basics. Flashy plays make the fans happy. Winning games makes them happier! The basics make them win. Any questions?

He focused on basics, and for years he dominated the game. Who do you think is going to dominate the sales game?

NATURAL SELLING CONCEPT #2

There are a million ways to do the basics, but by definition, there can only be one "best." And, the best changes over time. Tomorrow's best may be better than today's.

Are basics really all that important? Let me share a theory about what might have been if one of America's top corporations understood this.

In the early 1960s, IBM had a sales force that was the most professional and highly trained the world had ever seen. They understood that there were millions of ways to do things. But they also understood that there was only one best way.

This philosophy affected everything from their hiring to the clothes they wore. If you worked for IBM in the 1960s, you could wear whatever you wanted . . . as long as it was a dark blue suit, white shirt, dark tie and black wing-tip shoes. You had total flexibility to wear whatever you wanted as long as you followed those guidelines exactly!

IBM knew there was only one best way to dress, and they told their people, "If it's the best, we should all do it . . . If it's not the best, none of us should do it."

IBM salespeople wore flared pants in the Sixties but not wide bell-bottoms because wide bell-bottom pants were never the best. IBM salespeople never went through the leisure suit fad because leisure suits were never the best.

So, what happened to IBM in the 1970s?

Well, I don't know for sure, but I do know that styles changed and for some reason, IBM didn't. You see, up to that point, IBM had always stayed up with the latest styles. They knew that there was only one best, yet they also knew that the best continually changed.

Introduction

Maybe IBM's "best-way-to-dress police" retired or died. We don't know for sure, but we do know that when pink and purple shirts, long hair, and the casual look became the style, IBM went into a multi-year nosedive.

Through the late 1960s IBM attracted 99% of the top college graduates. They didn't hire them all, but they had their pick of the litter. After the early 1970s, it was no longer as fashionable to accept a position with "Big Blue" and the rest is history. IBM stopped being the best in other areas of technology and service about the same time. Draw your own conclusion. Mine's a theory.

I can also theorize that in the early 1970s, Bill Gates would have given his eyeteeth to have a million-dollar budget to play with bits and bytes and develop software for a powerhouse like IBM. But why would IBM hire a guy who looked like that? And why would Bill Gates want to work for a company like IBM that made you look like them?

The balance of this book is dedicated to showing you how to develop and maintain your own personal best way to sell using your natural style. There is a best way to plan a call, a best way to open a call, a best way to conduct a call, and a best way to close a call.

We are going to break the sales process down into each of its component parts. Then, we will look at the best way for you to do each part. Finally, your mission will be to make sure you are doing your best in each part naturally and continually looking for "better."

NATURAL SELLING CONCEPT #3

You can only be your best if you and your organization are committed to each of the following timeless values:
- *Honesty and integrity*
- *Caring for the people you work for and with*
- *Treating people fairly*
- *Delivering more than your customer expects*

DEFINITION

Webster Salesperson: The salesperson who exhibits one or more of the following characteristics: rude, crude, obnoxious, dishonest, pushy, arrogant, talks too much, listens too little, knows it all, wastes your time, wants your money but doesn't want to serve, feels you have his money in your pocket and his job is to get it, thinks it's okay to tell little white lies, thinks it's okay to tell big ones in full-color, etc., etc., etc.

In other words, the kind of salesperson who gives the profession a bad name; the kind of salesperson I hope you will never want to be; the kind of salesperson I hope you never *will* be!

Introduction

Typical definitions of sell, sold and selling — from several popular dictionaries . . . Check your own dictionary to see how it defines these words.

sell, sold, selling: 1) to give up, deliver, or exchange property, goods, services, etc. for money or its equivalent; 2) to have or offer regularly for sale; deal in a store that sells hardware, to sell real estate; 3) to give up or deliver (a person) to his or her enemies or into slavery, bondage, etc., to be a traitor to; betray (a country, cause, etc.); 4) to give up or dispose of (one's honor, one's vote, etc.) for profit or a dishonorable purpose; 5) to bring about, help in, or promote, the sale of; 6) to establish faith, confidence, or belief in; to sell oneself to the public; to persuade (someone) of the value of something; convince; 7) to cheat or dupe; 8) a trick or hoax; 9) to get rid of by selling, esp. at low prices; 10) to exchange one's services for a price, esp. for a dishonorable purpose, as for prostitution; 11) to get rid of completely by selling; 12) to betray (one's associates, cause, country, etc.); 13) to give up or be unfaithful to one's artistic aspirations or moral principles so as to achieve success, financial gain, etc.; 14) to value at less than its worth; underestimate; 15) to sell all of (the land or household goods) of (a debtor) so as to satisfy his or her debts.

Note: This is why I use the term "Webster Selling" to mean the wrong kind of selling.

Never allow your good to prevent you from becoming your <u>BEST</u>.

–C. Bromer

❧ CHAPTER ONE ❧
Theory

Why do people do the things they do? Why do decision-makers make the decisions that they make? It's hard to understand human behavior. In fact, my own behavior often confuses me.

Have you ever left a meeting, slapped your forehead and thought, "I can't believe I said that!" Or, "I can't believe I *didn't* say that!" Or, "Why did I *do* that?" These thoughts are usually accompanied by a sinking feeling in the pit of your stomach.

Saying or doing things that I regret is bad enough, but realizing that I do the same things again and again really hurts. It's as though my habits are controlling my actions.

Wait a minute! That's what habits are supposed to do! Habits cause people to respond to situations quickly and without thinking. Some are good, like brushing your teeth, and some are not so good, like biting your nails.

After years of study, I have come to the realization that the quality of your sales effort will be predetermined by the quality of your responses to fairly predictable situations. Your responses will be controlled to a large extent by the habit patterns that you have learned or allowed to develop.

We are creatures of habit. The way we tie our shoes . . . button our buttons . . . the language that we speak . . . and even the way we think. All of these things are controlled or significantly impacted by habit.

By definition, **a habit is an automatic response to a given stimulus.** If I ask for your name, you don't have to think about it. You have an automatic thought pattern and you automatically think or say your name. It's a habit. When you cross a street, even if it's a one-way street, you will look both ways. It's a habit. When I say, "Mary had a little . . ." You automatically think, *"lamb."*

Why?

It's a habit — a mental habit! It's an automatic, most-appropriate response to "Mary had a little . . ."

What does this have to do with selling?

Listen carefully!

When you're selling, you sometimes run into fairly predictable roadblocks or objections. People have fears that they might not make good decisions. Sometimes customers decide that they would rather deal with a competitor. Sometimes they decide not to deal with anyone. Sometimes they just don't like you.

An *objection* is any reason that a prospect gives for not going forward. In an ideal world, there would be no objections. However, they do happen and the only way to totally avoid them is to totally avoid other people!

You can't avoid objections . . . but you can be prepared for them if you have what I call a **"lamb"** ready for each one that comes up.

In other words, if you can respond to an objection as quickly, confidently, and appropriately with **the best possible response every time,** like your response to, "Mary had a little . . ." then you will sell more.

DEFINITION

Lamb: The most appropriate *(best)* response to any specific thing another person can say or do.

If you have a good response (a lamb) for everything a prospect can say or do, you will have more confidence and will likely achieve better results.

So why don't you currently have a lamb for everything a prospect can say?

Your first thought might be, "There must be millions of different objections. How can I possibly have a lamb for each one?"

Having a lamb for each objection (if there really were millions) would not be practical. However, later in this book I will prove to you beyond question that there really are very few objections; they are predictable and prospects are not inventing new ones!

If there really are very few objections and if they are predictable, then it becomes possible to develop good lambs for each.

What do you need to do?

1st   Break the sales process into its component parts.

2nd   Decide the best way to do each part.

3rd   List the objections that can happen in each part.

4th   Develop a good lamb to use for each objection that comes up.

5th   Commit these lambs to memory. (Be able to naturally respond.)

6th   Make more calls because it's more fun now that you're ready with good responses to the things that had slowed you down before.

7th   Enjoy more success than ever before.

Later, I will show you that you aren't memorizing "canned" or "mindless" responses. You're really preparing the best strategy or approach for each objection. Lambs can be approaches, strategies or the actual words you use.

Natural Selling Concepts

Why prepare strategies? Because objections like, "Your price is too high, I buy from one of my friends, I want to think it over, etc.," are predictable. You know you are going to hear them again and again. It's not a matter of whether or not you are going to hear them, it's only a matter of whether you will have a lamb ready when you do! Your success will be determined by how well you respond. If you have a lamb, you have a best response. Later, I will show you how to always have the best response.

Figure 1-1 illustrates the steps you go through in making decisions. Guess what? It's the same process your prospects go through when they make decisions.

Those whom we are trying to influence (prospects) also go through this process and they will make decisions based on how they interpret (filter) our words and actions. They evaluate and interpret our words and actions based on their current filter system. "Filter system" is synonymous with "value system."

Earlier, I stated you need to do seven things. The fourth on the list was, "Develop a good lamb to use for each objection that comes up repeatedly." I used the lamb illustration to help you understand the automatic nature of responding to objections and decision-making in general.

Having lambs is a necessary part of being your best in selling.

Before we leave this chapter on theory, let's have a quick look at the part of the diagram called subconscious. I will refer to this as a filter system since we all filter sensory input and make decisions based on this system. Your filter system is a combination of stored data, goals, desires, prejudices, likes, and dislikes. Your sales prospects each have their own unique filter system as well.

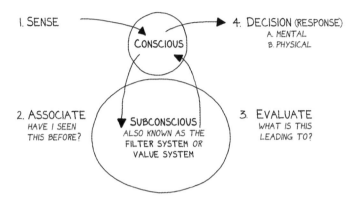

1. SENSE

CONSCIOUS

4. DECISION (RESPONSE)
A. MENTAL
B. PHYSICAL

2. ASSOCIATE
HAVE I SEEN
THIS BEFORE?

SUBCONSCIOUS
ALSO KNOWN AS THE
FILTER SYSTEM OR
VALUE SYSTEM

3. EVALUATE
WHAT IS THIS
LEADING TO?

1st step — We *sense* (hear, touch, taste, etc.) something.

2nd step — We look into our subconscious (our memory) and we *associate* the sensory input with what we already know.

3rd step — We *evaluate* what is happening in light of what we already know: Our past experiences; our habit patterns.

4th step — We make a *decision,* which always has a *mental aspect* and sometimes follows with a *physical action.*

Figure 1-1: Thought-Habit-Action Pattern*

This diagram breaks the thinking process into a logical step-by-step process.

* Special thanks to Mr. Lou Tice of: The Pacific Institute®, 1709 Harbor Avenue SW, Seattle, WA 98126.

The illustration used to explain our thinking pattern (Figure 1-1) was originally developed by Mr. Tice a number of years ago. It has been modified slightly and used with his permission.

You must understand your prospect's filter system in order to really understand his* needs.

You must know how to position yourself to be the solution for the needs that your prospects reveal. If your offer is properly positioned, your prospects will respond most appropriately and hopefully favorably.

If you do as most salespeople do, you may talk too much and never learn enough about your prospect's values to be able to accurately, appropriately, honestly and favorably appeal to them.

You don't want to manipulate your prospects. That's a Webster thing to do! You only want to make sure you are positioning your products and services in such a way that your prospect recognizes your offer(s) as legitimate and desirable. If your prospect dislikes salespeople who talk too much and listen too little, it would be desirable to know this before starting to tell him about your products or services.

And, by the way, most buyers do dislike salespeople who talk too much before listening. Ask yourself how you feel about salespeople who tell you all about what they're selling before they know your needs. In fact, you already have a lamb for these Webster salespeople. Don't you typically say, "No thanks!"

NATURAL SELLING CONCEPT #4

When your prospects nod their head, it doesn't mean *they're listening* or *agreeing*, it only means *you're* not listening . . . because you're talking!

Have you ever found yourself in a one-sided conversation with someone who is talking on and on and on? You are nodding your head and looking at them but not hearing

---

* For readability's sake, we've used the male pronoun rather than "he/she" "him/her." Your prospect is every bit as likely to be female, and you will want to adjust the scripts that appear in upcoming chapters accordingly.

a word they're saying. You might even be thinking to your-self, *How much longer is this windbag going to go on?*

They might believe you're listening because your eye contact, head nodding and occasional, "I see," has them fooled into thinking they're communicating, but you are not in the same conversation and might as well be in a different room.

The next time you are talking to someone who is nodding their head and saying, "I see," you might want to stop talking and start asking questions. At least confirm that they understand what you've been saying.

NATURAL SELLING CONCEPT #5

It's not what you know that counts! It's what your habits remind you to *say and do*.

When you do not have a lamb (a most appropriate response) ready to go, you must rely on your ability to "wing it." You may be good at winging it, and sometimes you may even say something good. However, more often than not you will say something less than your best.

To paraphrase, "Your challenge is to list all possible situations, list all possible objections, and then develop lambs (best approaches and best responses) for each. Then, know these lambs so well that they become natural, auto-matic, most appropriate best responses to situations and objections you are guaranteed to face."

That's your challenge. That's what *Natural Selling Concepts* is all about. That's what you are going to learn in the balance of this book.

The danger in the good times is that we develop habits that will not sustain us when times turn bad.

–C. Bromer

❧ CHAPTER TWO ❧
The *Natural Selling Process*

Many people believe you are a natural-born salesperson if you are outgoing, friendly, upbeat, a
prolific talker and have a knack for telling jokes.
While admittedly the sales profession is heavily populated
with this stereotype, it's also true that many good-inten-
tioned salespeople with these personality traits often fail for
lack of effective selling skills. The truth is you can be
extremely successful using your own style — a style that
comes naturally to you.

The title of this book is *Natural Selling Concepts*.
When you put the concepts to work in the real world, we
call it the *Natural Selling Process* — natural because you will
learn how to succeed in selling without changing your
personality, i.e. your natural style. You don't have to trans-
form yourself into a hyper-happy, super-slick, fast-talking
huckster to succeed. You can be successful just as you are.
What you will have to do is understand the selling process
— understand the concepts and principles that govern
success at each step — commit to be your best at each of
those steps — then practice the skills and get ready to enjoy
enormous success.

First, let's look at the process. Then in subsequent
chapters we will look at the concepts that govern sales
success, the commitment needed to excel at these steps, and
the skills you will need to develop and polish.

Selling is a contact activity and, therefore, requires
verbal skills and interpersonal (relationship-building) skills.

Skills can be learned in a classroom, but to implement

them proficiently you must practice them. Two of the highest-paid professions in the world are Hollywood actors and professional athletes. What do athletes and actors do when they aren't "playing?" That's right, the good ones are practicing or rehearsing. They know that when they are on the playing field or on the stage, there's a best way to perform. They want to know the part so well that they don't have to worry about what they are going to do . . . or when they are supposed to do it.

The athlete practices so he can concentrate more on the opposition and be ready to take corrective action if the opposition makes a sudden or unexpected move.

Actors can focus more on facial expressions and body movement if they have rehearsed their lines enough to do them "without thinking."

These actors and athletes have learned that if you want the whole process (i.e. the movie, the game) to be the best, you have to break it into component parts and make each part the best. Then practice each "best" part until it becomes second nature, or "natural."

The objective of the *Natural Selling Process* is to look at the total selling process, make sure we have addressed every distinct component of the process, and then decide the best approach for each part. Of course, there are many ways to undertake each step of a process — a few ways may even be worthwhile. Yet, there will only be one best way.

The component parts of the *Natural Selling Process* are shown in Figure 2-1 on the facing page.

On the surface, Figure 2-1 may appear complicated, but as you walk through it, you will find it to be remarkably simple.

The logical starting point is the upper left-hand corner.

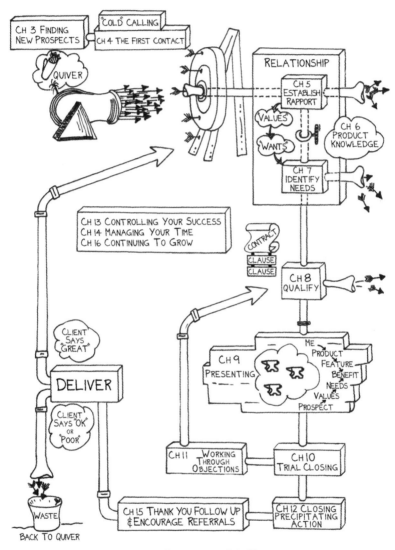

Figure 2-1: The Natural Selling Process

NOTE: The numbers in the blocks represent the chapters in this book
where the steps will be more fully analyzed.

Natural Selling Concepts

Prospecting is getting the names of people and companies who might have a need for your products or services. The "3" in the box tells you that prospecting is covered in more detail in Chapter 3.

Prospecting is the work you do before attempting to make contact and involves compiling company names, individual contact names, addresses, e-mail addresses, telephone numbers, etc.

Cold Calling (Chapter 4) is physically attempting to make the first contact with a prospect. This may happen via the telephone or in person. In either case, there are "best" ways to do each step in a cold call.

The arrows in Figure 2-1 represent prospects who have not yet been qualified — sometimes referred to as "suspects."

Building Relationships (Chapters 5, 6, and 7) involves many things. Building rapport, having good product knowledge so you can recognize needs, and having good communication skills are a few of the areas involved.

Qualifying (Chapter 8) is one of the most critical steps in the *Natural Selling Process*. If understood and done properly, it is the biggest time saver and the most effective aid to closing. When you understand and practice this natural best way to qualify, your productivity will skyrocket.

Presenting (Chapter 9). Most salespeople think this is what their job is all about. However, if you do everything correctly up to this point, the presentation is actually a fairly insignificant part of the selling process.

Trial Closing (Chapter 10) is testing the water before you jump in. It is a final step to see if there are any objections still lurking in the background before you attempt to close the sale.

Working Through Objections (Chapter 11) Objections are the reasons buyers give us for not going forward with the sale. You need to have a good lamb (a most appropriate response) for each objection that might come up. You will see in this chapter that the list of possible objections is really very short. You will also see that most salespeople generate their own objections and then fail to deal with them properly. In Chapter 11, you will learn how to prepare a lamb for every objection you might ever face.

Closing (Chapter 12) is precipitating action. It's asking or influencing the buyer to agree to take some action. I used to say, "If you don't close, you're just a professional visitor." But then one day, a friend reminded me that professionals get paid and amateurs do not. He said, "If you don't attempt to close, you're not even a professional visitor, you're an amateur visitor!"

Controlling Your Success (Chapter 13) is critical, especially in light of the fact that you do not control your results. Quality improvement is the only way to become the best, and continuous quality improvement is the only way to stay the best. You have to measure something to be able to manage it, so how do you measure a subjective thing like the quality of a sales call? The answer is the same one that helped the Japanese excel in the automotive industry. Break quality into its component parts and do your best to make each part at least a little better. Then, on a regular basis, ask yourself how each part can be made even better.

Time Management (Chapter 14) is a misnomer. Time is not manageable! It comes and goes at a constant rate and you can do nothing to affect it. However, you can manage and optimize the things you do with time. You manage what you do (Activity) and how well you do it (Quality).

Good time management in selling means optimizing the selling cycle. That's the time it takes to go from "Hello" to "Thanks for paying your bill." It might be minutes. It could be years. Good "time management" speeds up the cycle.

Follow-Up and Thank-You (Chapter 15) when done in the best way make even average products and services superior. In fact, some of the best relationships in business began with problems between salespeople and customers.

Is the Natural Selling Concepts *diagram (Fig. 2-1) the same for all opportunities, all prospects and all customers?*

Yes. It shows every part of the *Natural Selling Process.* The diagram does not change.

However, the number of steps you might use does change from call to call. You do not have to use all of the steps in every selling situation. If you walk into a buyer's office and the buyer says, "I'm glad you're here, I have an order to place," you won't say, "But I still need to make my presentation!"

You just use the steps necessary to complete your objective. Your objective is to find people who have needs that your products and services can satisfy and then fill those needs so you and your customer both make a profit or a gain.

Aren't all prospects (decision-makers) essentially the same?

No! Keep two things in mind.

First, from our chapter on theory, each decision-maker has a unique filter (value) system, which means each will perceive a different set of needs. Engineers are typically concerned with how something functions, purchasing people are more interested in price and delivery, and owners focus on corporate image, growth and return on investment.

Second, there are three different levels of decision-making in the selling process:

The Natural Selling Process

1. *Awareness:* At this level are decision-makers who are aware of you, but have never met you. They know a little about you but they don't usually buy from you. Your objective is to get in and find out what you need to do in order to start doing business.

2. *Acceptance:* These decision-makers may accept you and consider you, assuming you have the best price.

   They are prospects or customers who have no loyalty to you or your company and they may or may not have loyalty to one of your competitors. Your objective in this situation is to find out what you need to do to be their best supplier or provider and then initiate plans to do it if possible.

3. *Preference:* The third and best level of decision-makers are those who prefer you. These are people who will use you until you do something to damage your relationship. These customers will give you all of their business. They will tell you if a competitor tries to undercut your prices. They are your bread and butter, worth their weight in gold, and you must take excellent care of them. Your objective here is to make sure you continue to serve them by staying up to date on their evolving needs and then exceeding their expectations as you fill those needs.

NATURAL SELLING CONCEPT #6

You will have the least amount of competition when you achieve and maintain *preference.*

Your overall objective is to have as many good customers as possible at the preference level.

So, if the diagram is the same for all prospects, but each prospect is different, how do you become your best?

Just like playing baseball or tennis, you become your best through understanding and through the ability to execute the basics so naturally that you do them automatically. This leaves you more time for thinking and reacting to the variations in the process.

If you internalize the best activity for each step in the *Natural Selling Process,* you will be your best — naturally!

To illustrate, assume $1,000,000 is waiting for you at the Transamerica Pyramid in San Francisco (Figure 2-2) and all you have to do to claim the money is to show up in one week with a picture ID.

If that were true, would you be there?

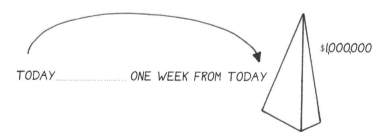

Figure 2-2: The Best Activity for Each Step

You wouldn't have to think about it very long! You would immediately, automatically know that you could be there. In fact, you would probably be there a day in advance with three or four picture ID's. You wouldn't have to think long because you already have internalized the process of physically getting yourself from where you are to anywhere in the world, given a reasonable amount of time.

When you have a process internalized, your habit patterns kick in and you don't even think about it. Your "auto-pilot" takes over.

That's what I want you to do with the *Natural Selling Process*. I want you to internalize it!

When a process is internalized, you have the best chance of succeeding.

NATURAL SELLING CONCEPT #7

You will achieve your best results when you do the best activity in each step of the *Natural Selling Process.*

The only thing better is to go one step further and INTERNALIZE the best activity in each step of the *Natural Selling Process*, so that it becomes second nature.

If you were on your way to the Transamerica Pyramid and you encountered a detour, you wouldn't become frustrated, turn around, and go home. You would get frustrated and keep on going. In fact the frustration would create energy that would help you to keep going.

Little setbacks are part of life. They may slow you down, but they don't have to stop you. They only stop you when you don't have the process internalized; when you don't know the best thing to do next!

Natural Selling Concepts

That's what I want you to be able to do when you're selling. I don't want little setbacks to stop you or even slow you down. Sure, they're frustrating. But if you have the best process internalized (the *Natural Selling Process*), the frustration will create a desire to press on and will even create the energy necessary to succeed.

❧ CHAPTER THREE ❧
Finding New Business . . . Prospecting

What is "Prospecting?"

Prospecting is obtaining the names of people and companies who should have a need for your products and services. It is the research portion of the sales process.

I have met salespeople who claimed to know all of the prospects in their area for their industry. Yet every salesperson can improve at prospecting.

In the late 1970s, The Osborne Corporation (which had pioneered laptop computer technology) had sales of over $100,000,000 when they filed Chapter 11 and vaporized. In that same period, Microsoft Corporation had ten to fifteen employees and a small fraction of Osborne's sales. Which would have been the better prospect if you were a salesperson for a shipping and retail display box company?

So, why do you need to prospect?

If you have been selling for over twenty years, you know the answer already! As a rule, 80% of your time and effort is spent servicing customers who make up 20% of your sales. Some of those low-revenue high maintenance accounts have great potential, which justifies the extra work. But if you are ever going to grow, you must constantly replace your lowest-revenue, lowest-potential, high-maintenance accounts with newer accounts with bigger potential.

That's why prospecting is important. Your chance of finding bigger and better prospects increases significantly if you have an active prospecting goal . . . and a plan.

There's another reason for prospecting. According to I-Market that specializes in selling business databases, 22% of all companies in the United States disappear every year. Yet, each year the total number of companies increases. This means every year approximately 2,000,000 businesses go under in America and every year more than 2,000,000 businesses are started.

In addition to current customers who go out of business, you will lose customers who form other friendships, leave the area, are sold, etc.

The fact is, even if you offer your products or services free, some of your current customers will not continue to work with you.

You need to generate a continuous supply of new "arrows" (Re: Figure 2-1) to insure a healthy business. Some of the arrows miss the target.

What are the best sources of new business?

Your best sources of new business are your current customers. There's a very good chance that your current customers don't use all of your services, and they may not even know of all the services that you can offer.

Try this exercise. (The longer you have been selling, the more frightening will be the results.)

First, list the top five things you sell. Be specific. Don't put service, quality and our people. Everyone sells those things. Put down specifically what you sell and do not cloud it with "sales talk" like investments in your future or high quality solutions or products that last.

Be specific! As an example, a list for my company might include:

1.   Business-to-business sales and sales management training.

2. Sales measurement and accountability system development and implementation.
3. Mentoring salespeople.
4. Field training (face-to-face) calling on real customers.
5. Sales and marketing plan development and long-range planning.

Construct your own list and take it with a $20 bill to one of your best customers. Place the list face down in front of the customer with the $20 bill on top.

Then, with the list, still face down, ask your customer the following:

"(Name), I'm doing a study to see how well we're letting our customers know everything we sell. Would you please help me? Would you please tell me what you believe are my actual top five products and services? I have them listed here and if you get all five correct, it means I'm doing my job, and it means you can have the $20 bill for your office coffee fund or petty cash account."

Use caution! Only do this with someone you know well. A stranger might consider it offensive. In addition, you must avoid the appearance of wrongdoing! Don't ever offer money under the table or to a person who might misinterpret what you are doing.

If you do this exercise properly, you will never give the $20 away. Even your best customers do not know the top five things you sell. Your customers are not out there memorizing what you sell.

What they think you sell may embarrass you. I did this exercise once with a very friendly, but relatively new, contact. This person who had bought from me in the very recent past actually named my competitor's brand name in his list.

Natural Selling Concepts

Your current customers are excellent prospects for two reasons. First, they don't know everything you sell. Second, they are the ones who will recommend you and refer you to others. They will always be your best source of new business. (This assumes you are doing a good job of serving their real needs.)

Remember our definition of selling is *finding people who have needs that your products and services can satisfy, and then filling those needs so you and your customer both make a profit or gain.* When your customer makes a profit or gain, you're filling real needs.

Your second best source of new business is new prospects with the same profile as your existing best customers.

The products and services you sell will appeal to companies and individuals who have common characteristics. If you can profile these common characteristics (size, age, structure, industry, business type, location, number of locations, etc.), you can then do research to find everyone in your marketing area who has a similar profile. Eliminate those companies and individuals that you are already working with and the rest should be very good prospects.

Three excellent resources for free research are your chamber of commerce, your library business department, and the Internet. However, your quickest and often most accurate (best) source for business profiling information is from companies who specialize in compiling statistical data for resale . . . companies like I-Market, Harris Info Source, Lazarus Research Group (www.lazresearch.com), etc. Other sources of free, but less focused, information are the Yellow Pages and newspapers.

Another highly rated prospecting tool is networking. It has been around since the Garden of Eden. The serpent got to Adam through Eve and made the sale to both. You might say the serpent was the first "Webster" salesman. He used networking (a good tool) to his advantage to sell a lie (a bad product).

Networking, by definition, is leveraging current relationships in either a business or social environment for the purpose of shortcutting and speeding up the selling process. It is using current relationships to help accelerate the building of additional relationships with new prospects.

It's a good way to secure leads, recommendations, and referrals. It is fairly time-consuming, but it can save months or even years in relationship building.

Summary

Prospecting is the first step in the *Natural Selling Process*. Whether you are new or have been selling for forty years, you cannot be your best in the whole process if you are not your best in every step.

What does it take to be your best?

Time and effort!

Develop a prospecting plan. First, start contacting all of your active and inactive accounts and go through the exercise to see if they know your top five products and services. Simultaneously, develop a profile of what your best prospects should look like (size, age, structure, industry, business type, location, number of locations, etc.).

Next, dedicate up to two hours each week to doing research. Your goal should *not* be to spend the *full* one to two hours. Your goal should be to get enough new prospects each week that you will never run out of new people or new businesses to call. The number of new sales calls you make each week determines the actual number of prospects you will need.

Make an appointment with yourself each week for the one to two hours and then protect the time just like you would for an important customer.

Make the commitment to be your best at prospecting.

❧ Chapter Four ❧
The First Contact . . . The "Cold Call"

C old calls can be useful in prospecting (gathering information) for the future and they are better than doing nothing between calls when you have extra time. However, your time is always best invested doing those activities first that give the highest payback.

Your priorities should be:

1st   Writing orders with active customers.

2nd   Developing active customers.

3rd   Getting appointments with qualified prospects.

4th   Making cold calls on the telephone and in person to start the qualification process. (Dropping in on someone "cold" is always an option, but your success percentage will typically be so low that you should do it only as a last resort.)

5th   Prospecting and paperwork that can be done before and after prime selling hours.

Some of the most prominent sales trainers in the world really bad-mouth cold calling. This is because they define cold calling as randomly calling anyone or dropping in on unqualified strangers without an appointment. This is not cold calling. This is *stupidity*.

The only good reason that I know for unplanned cold calls is to fill in unexpected free time and, again . . . the purpose is to start the qualification process.

Natural Selling Concepts

It is normal for as many as 20% of scheduled appointments to be cancelled or changed due to reasons beyond your control. Cold calls are a productive way to use this unexpected free time. Since cancellation is always a possibility, you should have alternate cold calls preplanned as much as possible.

Suppose you are one hour away from your office and your next appointment is in two hours. It doesn't make sense to go back to your office, and it doesn't make sense to waste time. Cold calling in this instance can be an excellent way to prospect for new business.

Professional cold calling is making new contacts (in person or on the telephone) with partially or prequalified prospects so you can qualify them. Prospects are qualified when you have confirmed that they have a need that your product or service can satisfy in a way that you and they will both make a profit.

There is a logical step-by-step sequence of events in typical first calls . . . You might think that you would need to master millions of different skills to be able to cover all of the possible first call scenarios. Actually, there are only seven. You may not need to do each one on each call, but you will never have to do more. The diagram in Figure 4-1 shows all of these possible scenarios.

If you have a best thing to say for each scenario, you are ready to make great cold calls.

The best thing to say in each situation is longer than a lamb so we call it an **elevator speech.** When someone asks you a question on an elevator, you only have ten to fifteen seconds to answer. An elevator speech is a "lamb paragraph," a *most appropriate response* to a situation, *and* it must be short . . . maybe two or three sentences.

Have an elevator speech ready for each of the scenarios

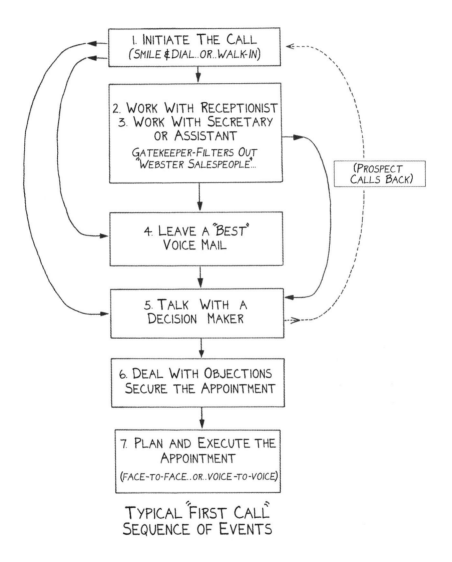

TYPICAL "FIRST CALL"
SEQUENCE OF EVENTS

Figure 4-1: Typical "First Call"

Sequence of Events

shown in Figure 4-1 . . . Have them internalized which means you can recite them automatically like "Mary had a little . . ." If you have one for each scenario, you will be ready for everything that can happen during a first call and nothing should surprise you.

You may walk in and be greeted by the decision-maker who immediately asks you to proceed with your call (steps 1, 5 & 7), or you may have to go through each step.

Let's walk through the steps and look at the best way to do each.

1. Initiate the call (Smile & Dial or Smile & Walk In):

Whether you are dialing on the telephone or entering a lobby, a smile is essential. It will improve your face. It will improve your voice and it will improve your prospect's response. Everyone likes being around "up" people. Nobody likes being around "down" people. Even your own family will avoid you if you're constantly down.

2. Receptionist

There are two possibilities when you make this first call. Either you know the name of the person you wish to speak with or you don't. If you know the name of the person you're calling, just ask to speak with him.

If you do not have the name of the decision-maker, the following approach (elevator speech) is the best:

"Hi, my name is _____; I'm with [company name]; would you please help me with a few names? [Do not pause] I usually work with the [Titles]: _____, _____, or _____. Would you please help me with their names so I can call for an appointment?"

The reason you should go for three titles is to improve the possibility of finding the best contact.

The First Contact . . . The "Cold Call"

This approach works the best for three reasons: First, you are asking for help. People are wired to give help. I have never heard anyone ever respond, "I'm sorry, I don't help people." Second, you are saying you are going to call for an appointment. Receptionists love salespeople who get appointments before they come in. Third, it shows respect and courtesy to the receptionist.

It still amazes me how many salespeople do not show common courtesies to receptionists.

Kathy (our receptionist at the time) once called me shortly after a salesperson left my office. She asked, "Who was that jerk?" I asked her to whom she was referring, and she described the salesperson who had just departed. She went on to say he was rude and arrogant to her and to another visitor in our lobby. That salesperson appeared to have a good product, but we never did business with him.

The script above is the best I know, but don't use it word for word. Put it into your own words! I have never advocated "canned" selling where you use someone else's words. "Planned" selling is best. Planned well enough that you know what you are going to say and how you are going to say it. Just be sure to use your own words and your own style.

3. Gatekeeper — secretary or assistant

There is a subtle difference between a receptionist and a gatekeeper. Receptionists will generally send you to voice mail or to the person you have asked for, or they might just take a message if the person you want is unavailable. Gatekeepers, by contrast, ask qualifying questions such as, "Is he expecting you?" or, "Does he know what it's about?" The gatekeeper and receptionist may be the same person, but you need to be ready for both.

When you are asked a qualifying question, you need to be ready with a lamb, a most appropriate response.

The best lambs I know for the most typical questions that gatekeepers ask are as follows:

(Q) *"Is he expecting you (your call)?"*
(A) "No, we haven't met. I just have a couple of quick questions for him. May I speak with him?"
(Q) *"Does he know what it's about?"*
(A) "No, we haven't met. I just have a couple of quick questions for him; is he available?"
(Q) *"Can I tell him what it's about?"*
(A) "Yes, I am in the _____ industry (or business), and I have a couple of quick questions for him; is he available?"

(Caution: The more information you give, the better your chances of not getting past the gatekeeper. Remember that the gatekeeper's function is to keep Webster salespeople out. (Initially, all salespeople sound like Webster salespeople.)

Most prospects do not sit in their office hoping their telephone will ring so they can talk with salespeople. Since good prospects are always looking for ways to save time, the more information the gatekeeper passes on, the better the chance the prospect will assume you are selling a "standard product" and then make two decisions. First, that their needs are satisfied and second, there is no need to see you or talk with you. There is a possibility that your prospect will be looking for exactly what you sell, but the likelihood is small. Do not try to sell your products or services to the gatekeeper, and do not be disrespectful in the process.

You must be prepared to answer additional questions. You may be asked:

(Q) *"Can you be a bit more specific?"*
(A) "Actually, you might be able to help me with the

first question: Is he the main contact in the
_____ area? [Fill this space with
one to three words that describe what you do or what
you sell. If it takes more than three words, rethink and
shorten it until you can describe it in three words or
less. Make a note of their response. Then continue.]
"What would you suggest as the best way for us to set
a time to show him (our product or what we do), or
talk with him briefly to see if it might be something
that would interest him?"
You may also be asked:
(Q) *"Can you send me something in the mail?"*
(A) [If you want to meet face to face] "We can bury
you with literature [if true], but it will save us a lot of
time if I could meet briefly and show him what we do.
Is he available to speak briefly on the telephone?" (to
set an appointment)
(A) [If you want to meet voice to voice] "We have
something to send, but it's not for everyone, and we
can bury you with literature that he might not be
interested in. Actually, it might save more of his time
if I could speak briefly with him. [Do not pause!] Is
this a good time to speak with him? [If no] Would you
recommend a better time for me to call back?"

4. Voice mail

Whether your call is taken by a receptionist, gatekeeper, coworker, or even if you make it all the way to your
prospect's telephone, you will often end up in voice mail.

There are millions of ways to leave voice mail. Some
are good. However, when you are leaving a voice mail for a
first contact, how many are *best?*

If you leave a typical Webster voice mail, you can
expect a callback rate of less than 1%. If you leave a *best*
voice mail, you have a much better chance for a callback —
perhaps as high as 35%. Keep in mind, we are talking
about getting callbacks from people who do not know you.

Natural Selling Concepts

A 35% callback rate is excellent. Even my wife doesn't return 100% of my calls!

One day, I made nine calls in a row to people I did not know. All nine of these calls resulted in my leaving a voice mail message. On the eighth call, something strange happened. When I hung up the telephone, I thought to myself, "Carl, you were awesome!" It was one of those calls where everything came out perfectly.

Every word!

Perfect!

Then I made the ninth call and everything I said came out wrong. The words were bad, the timing was bad, everything was bad! It just felt terrible.

That was when it hit me! The eighth voice mail message was awesome — It was the best — If I had left the same best voice mail for all nine, I would have had a better chance for nine callbacks.

What must you do to have a best voice mail response?

You must have a well-written, well-rehearsed, compelling sales script and you must answer your prospect's unstated question, "Why should I call you back?"

Experience and research have proven that the best voice mail has seven elements. Hundreds, perhaps thousands of salespeople have had the opportunity to refute or improve upon these seven steps. None have! Until that happens — and I am always open for improvements — these seven elements will stand as the best.

1. **Your name.**
    "Hi, Mr. _____, my name is _____."

2. **The name of your company.**
   "I'm with _____."
3. **Your telephone number.** *(Slowly! — People cannot hear on the telephone as fast as they can in person. This is because they have no visual cues like when listening face to face. Say your number slowly enough that you can write it down yourself as you speak it.)*
   "My number is: 800 [pause] 480 [pause] 5482."
4. **A brief comment acknowledging if you have ever met before.** *(People will automatically start wondering who you are. If you do not quickly identify yourself — in addition to your name — they may not continue to listen.)*
   "You and I have not yet met;" or, "You and I met at (a recent) trade show;" or, "We met briefly last week at (the Chamber of Commerce Business After Hours) . . . etc."
5. **An acknowledgment of where you got his name.** *(Same as #4 above — This will help people to understand who you are and why you are calling.)*
   "I got your name from (some research I've done); or, I got your name from (receptionist or gatekeeper's name) . . . etc."
6. **The purpose of your call — to get a call back.**
   Response: *(If you want to meet face-to-face)*
   "I would like to **show** you what we do and how we're different, but first, I need to ask a couple of quick questions . . ."

   Response: *(If you want to meet voice to voice)*

   "We have **something to send,** but before I send it, I need to ask a couple of quick questions . . ."

   The two quick questions: (a) "Are you the correct person?" and (b) "Is [*time & date*] a good time to [*meet/discuss*]?"

7. **A request for a callback and a restatement of #1, #2, and #3 above.** *(Again, slowly when you give your telephone number.)*
    "Would you please give me a call at your earliest convenience? Again, my name is _____, I'm with _____(Company), and my telephone number is _____."

Now, put it all together. Assuming you are trying to get a face-to-face appointment, this is what your voice mail speech might look like:

"Hello, Mr. _____, my name is _____, I'm with _____(company). My telephone number is _____. You and I haven't met yet; I got your name from:_____. The reason I'm calling is I'd like to <u>show you</u> what we do, and <u>how we are different</u>, but first, I'd like to ask a couple of quick questions. Could you please give me a call at your earliest convenience. Thanks . . . Again, my name is _____, I'm with _____(Co.), and my telephone number is _____."

On the other hand, if you are trying to sell on the telephone, it might look like this:

"Hello, Mr. _____, my name is _____, I'm with (company). My telephone number is _____. You and I haven't met yet; I got your name from:_____. The reason I'm calling is I'd like to <u>send you something</u> but first, I'd like to ask a couple of quick questions. Could you please give me a call at your earliest convenience. Thanks . . . Again, my name is _____, I'm with _____(Co.), and my telephone number is _____."

Three phrases are underlined above . . . <u>show you</u>, <u>how we are different</u>, and <u>send you something.</u> They are especially important if you want your prospect to have **the most appropriate response.**

The First Contact . . . The "Cold Call"

When people hear, "Mary had a little . . ." The most appropriate response is *lamb*. When you hear the words, "show you," it's most appropriate to want to have a look. It's not appropriate to say, "Send me something in the mail." It's also not as appropriate to say, "Tell me about it." If I use, "Show you," your normal response will be to want to have a "look" at it. When you hear the words, "How we're different," it's most appropriate to want to check me out. It's not appropriate to say, "I don't think I need your product or service." How could you know if you need my product or service? I already told you, "We're different!"

When you hear, "Send you something," it sparks curiosity and the desire we all have to receive things. It also implies that what I have to send is valuable, which is true! Even literature can be expensive and mailing it can be costly in terms of time and labor.

Those three phrases are important if you want your prospect to respond most appropriately.

You might be wondering if it's safe to just hang up when you start to hear a voice mail message. Not since the invention of "Caller ID." Even if you hang up, they are going to know you tried. And if you block your caller ID, everyone who has it will automatically assume you are a Webster telemarketer, and you will not get through even when they are there.

You may also be wondering how often or how soon you should try again if they do not return your call.

The answers to those questions are determined by the size of the sales opportunity. If the prospect is spending millions of dollars today, I might call back several times today! However, for most opportunities in most new accounts, a wait of seven or eight working days is probably about right.

Natural Selling Concepts

How many times you try is also a function of the sales opportunity. If you have been selling more than five years, you have probably heard many times that the average sale is made after five to seven "no's." Personally, I do not believe that is true.

Frank Bettger, in his best-selling book, *How I Raised Myself From Failure to Success in Selling*, said, "Seventy percent of my sales were made on the first interview, 23% on the second and 7% on the third and after."

Why spend large amounts of time going after low percentage results?

The late Harry Novick, who helped companies develop sales through manufacturing representatives, called business owners on a regular basis. He told me, "If they don't call back after the fifth call, I write them off. There are too many good prospects out there to waste time on people who will not show common courtesy by returning a telephone call. This assumes you have a planned voice mail, something to offer and you don't sound like a typical telemarketer."

The following scripts work well for me. Use your own words, but be careful about talking too much.

My 1st re-call attempt:

"Mr. Smith, this is Carl Bromer. I left a message for you last week and I do have a couple of quick questions to ask. If you could give me a callback at your convenience, I would greatly appreciate it. Again, my name is Carl Bromer, I'm with Stellar Sales Training, and my telephone number is: 800 (pause) 480 (pause) 5482."

My 2nd re-call attempt:

"Mr. Smith, this is Carl Bromer again. I've left a couple of messages for you and you are probably extremely busy or perhaps you have been out of town. I need to ask a couple of quick questions and would greatly appreciate a return call. My number is: 800 (pause) 480 (pause) 5482."

My 3rd re-call attempt:

"Mr. Smith, this is Carl Bromer. I have left several messages for you but for some reason, we haven't been able to get together. Let me give you my cellular number. [Give your cellular or home telephone number if it's important enough.] That number is: (give your number *slowly*) . . . Thanks, and I'm looking forward to hearing from you."

My 4th re-call attempt:

"Mr. Smith, this is Carl Bromer. I have left a number of messages, but have been unsuccessful getting together with you on the telephone. A week from Thursday, I plan to be in your area and would like to stop by to introduce my company and myself. I plan to be there at approximately 10:30 A.M. If that time is not good for you, would you please give me a call and let me know. You can reach me at _____ and again, this is (name and company)."

The first three re-call attempts are designed to get a call back without being a pest or giving too much information while at the same time projecting the confidence of a company owner with something important to ask.

The fourth attempt is actually setting a default appointment. The prospect must call back, or by default, we have an appointment. This is not recommended if you must travel very far because there is still a 50% chance the prospect will not come out to meet you when you show up. Nothing works all the time!

There is another option if you do not receive a call

back. After you leave your message, dial "0," ask for customer service, PR or vendor relations. They are normally in, do not typically have built-in sales resistance, and are often happy to help.

5. Talk with the decision-maker

Assuming you have made it through the receptionist-assistant-voice mail gauntlet, now you get to talk with someone who might be able to say, "Yes!"

First, you need to introduce yourself and quickly explain why you are calling.

"Mr. _____, my name is _____, I'm with (company name). Is this an okay time for a couple of quick questions?"

> No — *Ask when a better time would be for a call back.*
> Yes — *Proceed.*

"Are you familiar with our company?"

> Yes — *Stop and probe. (You have just jumped ahead to the need-finding step in the sales process.)*
> No — *Proceed.*

"We (complete description of what your company provides). I would like to stop by to actually **show** you what we do and **how we're different**. I believe you will be interested, and after a quick look, we'll know for sure. Then, if you're not interested, I'll be on my way or perhaps you could point me in a better direction. Would you be available (time/day)?"

If your prospect is returning your voice mail you can start in the middle by saying:

"Thank you for calling back, as I mentioned in my message, I have a couple of quick questions."

Question #1 asks if the prospect is the correct decision-maker. My first question:

"When it comes to making decisions about _____,
are you the best person to see? "

Question #2 asks when a good time would be to get
together.

"(Name), I would really like to **show** you what we do
and **how we're different.** How does (date/time) look
for us to get together?"

Have a lamb ready if the answer is still, no. You might
consider, "I don't blame you for not wanting to waste time
. . . my time is valuable too . . . It will only take a moment
or two to see if it's worth proceeding . . . Is there a better
time for you when we can briefly meet (talk)?"

Words like **"show"** and **"see"** are the best words to use
if you are reasonably sure you are talking with the correct
person and your goal is to get an in-person appointment. If
you want to continue on the telephone, change the "show"
to "discuss."

**6. Deal with objections (if necessary) and secure the
appointment.**

When you ask to set a time for an appointment, there
are only three possible answers. However, there are millions
of ways those answers can be stated.

The first answer is, *"Yes."* The second is, *"Okay, but
how about a better time?"*

The third is, *"No, I don't want to waste time."*

Every answer to a request for an appointment is actually a form of one of these three statements and only one is
an objection.

If they say, "Yes," proceed with the appointment.

If they say, "This week is not good . . ." or, "I will be
out of town that week . . ." or, "I'm really going to be tied
up for the next several days..." They are not objecting.
They are really saying, "Yes, but how about a better time?"

If they say, "I'm not interested . . ." or, "I already have a supplier . . ." or, "My (relative) sells this . . ." or, "Call back next year . . ." then, they are objecting! They are really saying, "*I don't want to waste time!*"

Any objection from a first contact should be treated as a stall objection.

All stall objections can be paraphrased, "*I don't want to waste time.*" Therefore, you only need one lamb. You only need one best response and I suggest:

> "Mr. _____, I can appreciate your not wanting to waste time. It will only take a few minutes to have a <u>look</u> at what we do and <u>how we're different.</u> Then, (1) if we can't both benefit, I will be the first to say we should not work together, or (2) if you are not the right* person, perhaps you could point me in the right direction. How does (date/time) look for you?" *(Be ready with your lamb if it's not a good time.)*

> (*Caution, do not say, "If you are not the right person," if you already know he is.)

7. Execute the appointment. (Make the first call and secure the order if possible.)

I am going to assume that you are making a first call, face to face, on a prospect. If your first call is voice to voice, it will be essentially the same.

You might be tired of hearing this, but it's critical to your understanding the simplicity of the *Natural Selling Process.* How many best ways are there to do a first call?

That's right!

There is only one!

The best first call, in my opinion, is the one that most quickly gets the prospect talking about his needs. Remember, we find needs and then fill them. To find real needs, we must listen.

The First Contact . . . The "Cold Call"

The best first call should have the prospect doing most of the talking within ninety seconds of the start.

If you have not already done so, now is the time to complete your prioritized list of products and services. In Chapter 3, I asked you to list the top five things you sell. You were to list specifically what you sell and not cloud it with "sales talk" like investments in your future or high-quality solutions or products that last. If you have not created your list, do it now! There's only one best list for what you sell. Don't call on anyone until you have decided what you sell and what your priorities are.

If your company has not already provided this list, then develop it now.

Assuming you have your list, you are now ready for the voice-to-voice portion of the sales call. Figure 4-2 shows the best first call (voice-to-voice portion) I have ever seen. Follow the same basic format, whether you are selling in person or on the telephone.

This best first call is designed to get your prospect talking so you can start to identify needs.

Once you have identified needs that your products and services can satisfy, you will need to re-qualify the decision-maker and the decisioning process. Typically, the bigger the project, the more complicated the decisioning process. We will go into more on this in Chapters 7 and 8.

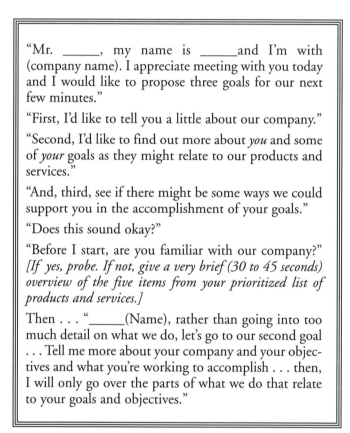

"Mr. _____, my name is _____and I'm with (company name). I appreciate meeting with you today and I would like to propose three goals for our next few minutes."

"First, I'd like to tell you a little about our company."

"Second, I'd like to find out more about *you* and some of *your* goals as they might relate to our products and services."

"And, third, see if there might be some ways we could support you in the accomplishment of your goals."

"Does this sound okay?"

"Before I start, are you familiar with our company?" *[If yes, probe. If not, give a very brief (30 to 45 seconds) overview of the five items from your prioritized list of products and services.]*

Then . . . "_____(Name), rather than going into too much detail on what we do, let's go to our second goal . . . Tell me more about your company and your objectives and what you're working to accomplish . . . then, I will only go over the parts of what we do that relate to your goals and objectives."

Figure 4-2: The Best First Call
Once you are face to face or voice to voice

CHAPTER FIVE

Establishing Rapport . . . Building Relationships

"Our business is different!"

This is the most common thing you will hear when you ask people to tell you about their business. Often, they will continue: "We're not like other companies. Our business is built on good relationships with our customers."

News flash! Each year, 78% of all companies in America are built on good relationships! Each year, the other 22% go out of business!

All businesses in a free enterprise system are built on good relationships. I have yet to see one that was not! When people have a good relationship in business, it typically means they like each other and they trust each other. Building a good relationship and having good rapport are critical because people buy from people they like and trust.

Being liked is important, but being trusted is critical. You will buy from people you trust, even if you don't like them. However, you will avoid buying from people you do not trust, even if you love them.

When you first meet someone, you mentally store him or her in your subconscious. (Earlier, we called this your filter system.) Actually, you store a mental picture along with your memory of the interaction. Every time after that, whenever you see, hear, or even think about that person, you will add to what you have stored. Each such incident will be positive, neutral, or negative. The more positives you store, the more you will like and trust that individual or company. The more negatives you store, the more you will dislike and distrust them.

These positives and negatives add up to form your relationship account balance. When you and the other person or company build a positive relationship account balance, you are building rapport.

If you are buying something and two or more people are selling that same thing, you will be inclined to buy from the one with whom you have the higher account balance. You will also be more inclined to recommend that person if the opportunity arises.

What is the best way to build a relationship with a new prospect?

Again, relationship is a combination of like and trust.

You build trust by meeting or exceeding the other person's expectations. You set those expectations early in the sales process by what you say and do and how well you say and do it. The best way to build "like" is on a foundation of trust. In other words, develop trust first and then build personal relationships on top of that trust.

This is the opposite of how most Webster salespeople operate. They believe getting the prospect to like them is the key, and they typically start calls with, "Hi, (Jim), I'm (Tom), how are you today?"

Greeting a prospect with these words is like having "I'm a Webster salesperson" tattooed on your forehead.

Then they typically go into twenty minutes of small talk because they mistake the prospect's hospitality and courtesy for an interest in them and their products and services.

If you want the prospect to trust you and eventually like you, don't waste his or her time by beginning with small talk! If your prospect wants to make small talk, that's okay; but always let your prospect lead in the small talk area. Allow the prospect to set the social tone of the sales call.

Natural Selling Concept #8

The best way to build trust with a prospect *before* the first order is to follow the *Three B's of Sales Etiquette:*

1. Be Brief — Have a plan before you make the call.
2. Be Bright — Know your products and services.
3. Be Gone — Leave before they wish you did.

Be Brief — There's only one best way to make a first in-person call or appointment. Have a plan before you call. Don't waste your prospect's time by being unprepared, and don't make small talk when that was not the stated purpose of your call. If the prospect wants to make small talk, then okay! Use your best judgment. However, don't initiate small talk unless you want to make them nervous. Don't start talking about the prospect's knickknacks or pictures . . . they might have higher priorities than your small talk. You could actually make them upset and never even know about it.

This is not to your benefit.

Rambling aimlessly, talking about your products or services is just about as bad.

In Chapter 4, you saw an outline of a best first call.

Remember, the best thing you can do in a first appointment is to get the prospect talking about his or her needs. How can you even begin to explain how your products or services will fill their needs before you know if there even is a need? *(More on identifying needs in Chapter 7 and planning calls in Chapter 15.)*

Be Bright — Know your products and services and the benefits that your products bring. Know the questions to ask so you can determine if your products and services can help your prospects support accomplishing their goals or solving their problems. *(More on product knowledge in Chapter 6.)*

Be Gone — Leave before your prospect wishes you did. Note: If you have difficulty getting back in to see someone after the first or second call, you may be staying too long and wasting their time.

How much time should you expect to invest in a first call? A good rule of thumb is to take less time than you requested when you set the appointment. If you asked for ten minutes, start with a plan that can be accomplished in less than ten minutes and then stop in ten minutes or less. If you asked for two hours, start with a plan that can be accomplished in less than two hours and then stop in two hours or less. *(More on planning calls in Chapter 15.)*

The best way to follow the three B's is to start each call (if the prospect doesn't start first) by clearly stating your purpose or objective for the call.

The best start might sound something like this: "Thanks for meeting with me today. I have three (four, five, etc.) goals that I would like to accomplish today. These are (list of goals). Are there additional goals that you might like to accomplish?"

The best way to build a relationship with customers after the first order is to continue to follow the *Three B's of Sales Etiquette.* Continue to come in with a plan that includes good questions based on sound product knowledge. Continue to use the prospect's time wisely and productively.

Do these things and you will continue to build a relationship with your prospect who will become your customer who will start to trust you and be on the way to becoming a friend.

What are some of the other factors that influence rapport and relationship building?

Establishing Rapport . . . Building Relationships

Everything you say, everything you do, and everything you are, affects your success in building rapport and relationships.

I will touch on twenty-five of these things later *(Chapter 14)*, but for now, you need to be especially aware of seven factors that will significantly impact your initial relationship building with new acquaintances.

1. Your clothing

Is there a *best* way for a salesperson to dress?

Styles change every day. Best today may not be best tomorrow.

Let me give you some guidelines that have served me well down through the years. These same guidelines are based on sound principles that do not change, so they should be good for years to come.

A. *Dress so your prospect will not remember what you wore.*

If your clothing is noticeable enough to detract your prospect's attention from what you are saying, it is probably not appropriate.

Conservative dress offends no one. Non-conservative dress is a distraction at best and can even be offensive to some people.

B. *Dress like the person your prospect goes to for advice.*

People go to bankers, lawyers, consultants, and other executives — people they respect — for advice. These advisors do not typically dress like vacationers. They dress sharp! They dress a cut above.

Dress conservatively, but dress a cut above. It's always easier to remove a tie or scarf and possibly roll up your sleeves than it is to dress up if you start out too casually.

Natural Selling Concepts

C. *Don't dress like your prospects dress.*

If you dress like they do, they may not see you as the expert.

Prospects want to buy the *best* value. What perception will your prospect have about the value of your product or service if you do not look like an expert? Your product will be judged by the way you look. Look sharp!

It is said, "Don't judge a book by its cover," but we do. You are the cover for your company.

2. Your smile

You've heard it before. You will hear it again. A smile is essential. It improves your face, your voice and your prospect's response. A smile may not get the order for you, but a frown or a flat expression can sure lose one.

Most people think they are good natural smilers.

Most people are wrong.

A natural smiler is a person who has a happy face — all of the time. Some people are said to have charisma. The most predominant characteristic of people with charisma is their warm, natural full-face smile. They are attractive and, in a friendly way, their appearance invites you to like them and trust them.

Some people only smile with their lips. You can tell it's not sincere. If you "take a lousy picture," there's a good possibility that you never learned how to naturally smile with your full face. Many small and otherwise very cute children, who pose for the family snapshot, look terrible as they distort their faces to "smile" for the camera. Most adults do the same thing; it's just not as noticeable.

You might think that a smile should be sincere and I agree. However, sometimes you just don't feel happy. Sometimes, you just don't feel like smiling. At times like those, pretend to be happy!

Establishing Rapport . . . Building Relationships

Zig Ziglar once said, *"I would much rather be around an insincere happy person than a sincere grouch."*

I strongly suggest the following exercise to help you determine the kind of smiler you are and then help you to develop a great natural full-face smile if you are in the majority of the population who have never learned.

First, stand in front of a mirror that's attached to a wall. You will need both of your hands to hold a book or some other object between your face and the mirror.

Look into the mirror and keep your eyes open and then completely block your reflection with the book. Now, with your eyes open but your view blocked by the book, get what feels like a really warm and friendly "look" on your face. It's important to keep your eyes open and your face "comfortable." Stabilize your face. Hold that feeling and then, without changing any facial muscles, lower the book or object and have a real look at your "warm and friendly" smile.

Most of the people who do this exercise will be surprised at how unfriendly they actually look compared to how they feel. If you look marvelous when you lower your book, you probably do not need the next exercise.

If you want to develop a great smile, do the exercise in reverse. Look into the mirror and use all of your facial muscles (eyes and forehead too) to develop a picture that you like . . . one that looks sincerely warm and friendly.

Without changing any of those muscles . . . put the book back between you and the mirror so you can't see your face and memorize the feeling. Memorization requires repetition, so you should expect to have to do this on several different days before becoming proficient.

As you become successful, expect those closest to you to notice a difference. They might say something or you might notice a change in their response to you. At the very least, you personally will notice a difference and don't be surprised if you start feeling better about yourself.

Smiling is critical! Even your own family will tend to avoid you if you're constantly down, and a smile attracts everyone except your competitors. It makes them nervous and it makes them wonder what you're up to. That's another good reason to smile!

3. Your neatness

Your business card, your car, your briefcase, your office, your personal appearance, your handwriting, everything about you, creates an image of neatness or an image of messiness. ("Messies" are sometimes referred to as slobs, though not usually to their faces!)

You can find out if you are a messy by asking someone who loves you to rate you on a scale of one to ten. If they feel you are a neat freak, they should give you a ten. If they feel you are a messy, they should give you a one.

Once they give their score, subtract three. If you are left with a five, you are on the bubble. If you are a four or less, you are dangerously close to being a slob, but don't expect your loved one to agree out loud.

If you believe being messy will not affect your business, ask yourself how you feel about shopping in messy, cluttered stores, or eating in messy restaurants, or getting your teeth cleaned by someone with an untidy appearance.

Several suggestions concerning neatness:
A. *If you have to straighten out your business card, don't give it out.*

Your business card should be pristine. A dog-eared messy card tells people that your products and services are probably dog-eared and messy as well.

B. *Have your car detailed (really, really clean) at least once per week.*

    You will feel better and any client who sees or rides in your car will also feel better.

C. *Keep your briefcase neat and never put it on a prospect's desk.*

    In fact, having one wide open on the floor or your lap is just about as bad.

    The best type of briefcase opens from the top. (Two examples are shown below in Figure 5-1.) This style allows you to reach inside more easily than the normal "clamshell-style" briefcase. They are easier to use if you are sitting or standing.

    Best briefcases allow you to easily retrieve material without cluttering your prospect's desk and without exposing everything you own.

Figure 5-1: Top-opening Briefcases are Best

D. *Invest non-prime selling hours to keep your office organized and neat.*

You should spend prime selling hours with prospects in person or on the telephone . . . not in your office. Prime selling hours are those hours when your prospects are most available, and they vary with different industries. If your typical prime selling hours are between 8:00 AM and 5:00 PM, you might consider an hour or two on Saturday mornings or maybe one evening each week to neaten up your office.

A neat environment will help you to be more productive, and you will be more confident when you feel better about your surroundings.

A clean desk is a sign of organization. A salesperson who can get good sales results and keep their work area neat is the kind of salesperson who gets promoted.

E. *Clothing does not make the person, but it sure helps to make the first impression.*

The best way to dress was covered earlier in this chapter. Just remember that your clothes will start talking about your professionalism before you speak a word. Make sure your attire is clean, pressed, and properly fitting your body.

F. *If your grammar is weak, if you are not an awesome speller, if your handwriting is poor, get help!*

Your written communication tells as much about you as your clothing. I once received a letter from a college graduate who said, "We was going to ship earlier, but . . ." My opinion of this person's products, services, and company took a nosedive.

G. *Check yourself in a mirror before leaving your home in the morning and after every meal.*

A piece of broccoli between your two front teeth will not impress anyone. There are numerous horror stories about salespeople who did not check their appearance in a mirror before making sales calls.

I know of one man who made sales calls all day and probably met twelve to fifteen prospects before he realized that his tie was left untied from when he dressed earlier that morning.

I know of another man who made several calls one afternoon after a lunch meeting. Returning home later in the evening, he found a pea from that day's lunch lodged in his beard!

These stories may sound silly, but it happens more often than you know. If you have been selling for more than a year, it has probably already happened to you.

Now, for the bad news — Nobody will tell you! You are on your own.

Make it a personal rule to never leave home or a restaurant without first examining yourself in a mirror.

4. *Your attitude* (projecting confidence)

The attitude that others perceive you to have will pull them closer or push them away. It needs to pull them closer! The best way to do this is to be positive, optimistic, decisive, and enthusiastic, just like an owner.

Owners tend to give prospects confidence in their company and its products and services. Confidence precedes trust and you need prospects to trust you. You need to give prospects confidence in your company and its products and services.

If you do this correctly, you will even give some prospects the perception that you are the owner.

This doesn't mean you have the owner's authority to make whatever decisions you want. It means you function in the prospect's eyes with the same credibility as if you were the owner.

For example, assume a prospect called and wanted to place a multi-million dollar order, but needed assurance that the work would be done in record time. An owner would say, "Let me check with my people to make sure we can make that. If we can, do you want to go forward?"

An owner wouldn't say, "Yes!" without checking with his people to make sure he could keep the commitment. That would be irresponsible and possibly financial suicide. Hasty commitments and knee-jerk promises destroy the prospect's confidence and trust.

Now, here's the real question for you: Is there anything better that you could say than what the owner said? Can you also say, "Let me check with my people to make sure we can keep a commitment like that, and if we can, do you want to go forward?"

How many best ways are there to respond to a prospect who is asking for a major commitment?

There are several words you should *not* use if you are trying to raise your prospect's confidence and trust levels. When you use words like "my boss," "my supervisor," "my manager," or "my superior," you are lowering your perceived importance in the prospect's eyes. Don't lie or deceive. That's a Webster thing! But don't create the wrong impression that you're unimportant by using those words.

Don't say, "I need to check with my boss."
Do say, "I need to check with my people."
Don't say, "I'm not authorized to make that commitment."
Do say, "Let me check with my people. If we can make that commitment, are you ready to go forward?"
Don't say, "My supervisor didn't approve it."
Do say, "I'm unable to approve this."
Don't say, "I don't have the authority to do that."
Do say, "Let me check this out and get back to you."
Don't say, "My manager will need to approve this."
Do say, "Let me check one thing before I approve this."
Don't say, "I will need to call the owner to see if . . ."
Do say, "Let me make a quick call to see if . . ."

Earlier, you were given two of the most significant parts of your job description as a salesperson. Finding people who have needs (prospecting and developing relationships) and then filling those needs (closing) in such a way that you and your prospect (now customer) both make a profit.

Now you have the third part of your job description, which is critical to the success of the first two.

NATURAL SELLING CONCEPT #9

Your job as a salesperson is to accomplish the following:

    a. Find People — People and companies who have needs that your products and services can satisfy.

    b. Fill Needs — Fill the needs of the people and companies in such a way that everyone involved makes a profit or gain.

Then, as you are finding people and filling needs, remember to . . .

> *c. Function as the Owner — Your attitude should be the same as that of an enthusiastic owner.*

5. Your odor

Believe it or not, this needs to be in this book. I'm sure you are a professional or you wouldn't be reading this. However, you also know that some people have blind spots. By definition, a blind spot is something you can't see.

There are three areas where you have to be careful about blind spots: body odor, breath odor and colognes or perfumes. Trust me, you will not do your best if you have a blind spot in any of these areas.

First, how do you know if you have body odor?

Even your closest friends will not tell you, and we know from people who have it that they are often oblivious.

So how do you discover if it's a blind spot?

Well, the next chance you get, in the privacy of your own home, and probably best done alone, take the clothing that has been closest to you all day. Roll it up in a ball and bury your face in it. Now you will know what your friends, coworkers and prospects know. Hopefully, it will not be an unpleasant experience.

It's probably a good idea to repeat this exercise on a regular basis.

Second, how do you know if you have bad breath?

If people back away or turn away on a regular basis, that's a hint.

If their eyes open wide for no apparent reason or if they gesture, like they're exhaling cigarette smoke but they aren't smoking, then you should take a hint.

Diet and health both contribute to the quality of your breath. Rather than trying to figure it out, carry and use breath mints. Avoid foods that you know cause problems. Brush your teeth throughout the day and have them professionally cleaned on a regular basis. Follow the rules your mother gave you when you were a child. Enough said!

Third, how do you know if colognes and perfumes are positive or negative?

Colognes and perfumes are infinitely better than B.O. or bad breath. However, unless you sell it, it's probably safer to avoid using it. Some people (prospects and customers) are even allergic to perfumes and colognes. I have never heard of a big sale being made because the salesperson smelled good.

If you do insist on wearing it, how much is the right amount? The best answer I ever heard came from an image consultant who attended one of our sales training programs. She said, "If you smell your own cologne or perfume anytime beyond the first minute or two, it's probably too much."

6. Your "bad" habits

Okay, now we're going to get personal. My intent is not to insult you or put you down, but to have you see things like other people see them. Then, make changes where necessary. Changes that will be beneficial to you, your prospects, and your career.

Four things can hurt you significantly more than they can benefit you. They are smoking, drinking, swearing, and driving distractions.

Smoking — Don't do it! Over 25% of the population will actually look down on you if you smell like cigarettes. If you call on companies that allow smoking, do it at the end of the day when you will not be visiting more prospects.

Smoking will not make sales for you. Have you ever

heard of anyone buying from a salesperson because they smoked? Even the cigarette companies do not buy from vendors because they smoke.

Not long ago, I did an experiment at a sales seminar in Chicago. I asked all of the non-smokers to stand up. There were over one hundred people present and at least three-fourths stood. Then I asked all those who would allow someone to smoke in their office to remain standing and those who would not allow someone to smoke in their office to sit down. About two-thirds sat down. Those still standing (non-smokers) were essentially saying, "I don't smoke, but you can go ahead and light up in my office if you want." Next, I asked all those who were still standing to raise their hand if the smoking would definitely bother them, but not enough to say something to the smoker. Almost every hand went up!

The biggest danger caused by smoking is offending the prospect or client and never knowing it.

Drinking — Having a drink during lunch demonstrates bad judgment. It will not help you to drive or think better. Don't do it!

Having a drink with a prospect or client in the evening will also not help you to drive or think better. Alcohol does not make you sharper mentally or more attractive. It might make you *think* you're mentally sharper and more attractive, but self-delusion is not the same as self-improvement. Don't do it!

If you entertain clients in the evening, ask yourself if a glass of anything with alcohol in it will make you sharper. Then ask yourself if being your best is important.

In over thirty years, I have personally been aware of a number of good people who have lost their jobs or clients because they drank. I have also heard of good people who lost their fortunes, their families, their freedom and in some cases their lives because they drank. I have never heard of anyone making a sale because they drank. Don't do it!

Driving distractions — Radios, electric razors, make-up, cell phones, CD players, etc.

Death can have a significant *negative* impact on your career! The amount of time you save will not have a significant *positive* impact on your career.

I know my comments here are not going to have a significant impact on driving habits and safety, but if it helps you for one day to avoid one bad situation, it's worth it. Please! Anything that can distract you should be taken care of before you start.

A word about cell phones: Many people are extremely offended or even become angry when they see people driving while talking on the telephone. I personally don't know of anyone who is impressed by this habit. When you are on your cell phone and have a prospect or client in your car or if one sees you driving, you will offend a certain percentage!

Keep in mind, this chapter is about building relationships through building trust. It's your choice. Choose wisely! If you make bad choices you will damage or even lose relationships.

7. Your enthusiasm and sincerity

Enthusiasm is the outer evidence of inner optimism. It is a great character quality to have because it attracts people. Pessimism, by contrast, pushes people away.

Where exactly, does enthusiasm come from?

"It's said that enthusiasm has sold more than all other things combined, but it was confidence that caused the salesperson to react with enthusiasm and it was competence that gave him the confidence. The truth is that competence has sold more than all other things combined, but it is 'enthusiasm' that gets the credit." –John Lawhon

Natural Selling Concepts

Having competence will help you develop enthusiasm, but many competent people are unenthusiastic and seem to accomplish little. So enthusiasm must require more than competence.

I believe that real, lasting enthusiasm comes from first having an exciting personal goal (whether it's for business, family, self, service to others, or whatever), and then having the *competence* and *drive* to accomplish it.

The purpose of this book is to help you build competence in selling and confidence that you know the best way to do it. Then, in Chapter 14, you will see the best way to set and achieve goals (great goals that will drive you to success) followed by the best way to organize your time, your territory, and your accounts.

Early in this chapter, I said, "All businesses in a free enterprise system are built on good relationships, and good relationships exist where people like and trust each other."

The best way I know to get people to like and trust you can be condensed into one Golden Rule — Treat others the way you would want to be treated. Obviously, this is not my original idea, but it's the best I know.

A good way to work with coworkers, prospects, and customers is to consider how you would interact with them if you were closely related. Most people have no trouble treating their family appropriately. Treat your customers the same. (This assumes, of course, that you love your family.)

Also, this does not mean you will give away your products or services free. If I'm selling to my brother in business and he's buying for his company, he knows I have to make a profit and I know that he has to receive good value. We can both win if we work together and if we have a good relationship.

NATURAL SELLING CONCEPT #10

Treat your customer as though he or she were your father or mother or brother or sister or son or daughter . . . Assuming you love these people! *(If you do this, you will be treating people the way you would want to be treated . . . AND . . . You will be treating them the way they want to be treated.)*

Whenever prospects have alternatives,
relationships are critical.
Prospects in a free enterprise system
<u>always</u> have alternatives.

–C. Bromer

❧ CHAPTER SIX ❧

Product Knowledge

Product knowledge is one of the most important elements in selling. It is represented in the *Natural Selling Process* diagram (Figure 2-1 and Figure 6:1) as a stopcock and is located in front of the "Identify Need(s)" block. Just as a stopcock regulates the flow of fluid through a pipe, so also product knowledge will regulate the flow of progress in the sales process. Stopcocks allow maximum flow when fully open, and they restrict flow when partially closed. Stopcocks do not create the flow. They only regulate it. Product knowledge does not create sales, but it can significantly regulate or diminish sales if you do not have it or if you do not use it properly.

Product knowledge training is a major problem area for many companies, and the reason might surprise you. Businesses approach product knowledge training with the misguided belief that being an expert in product knowledge will generate sales. More often than not, it only generates prolific and boring talkers. The stopcock doesn't generate the fluid. It only regulates it!

Having product knowledge (even in abundance and with perfect recall) does not guarantee success or generate

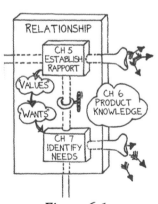

Figure 6-1:
Product Knowledge
Regulates Progress

sales. If it did, your top salespeople would be your employees with the most product knowledge; that is, product developers, engineers, and other cerebral types. It's been my experience that most of these "non-salespeople" would rather nail their tongue to a tree than make a sales call.

Product knowledge is important if you want to talk about your product or service. It's also important if you want to educate your customer. But selling is more than talking or teaching. In fact, a videotape can do a better job of both.

You aren't paid to talk and you aren't paid to educate. You are paid to discover your prospect's needs and then match those needs with your products and services in such a way that you both make a profit or a gain.

How should you use it?

When you think of product knowledge, there's probably no occupation in the world where it is more essential than in the medical profession. Product knowledge is critical for doctors, but how do they use it? They don't use it to educate you or to teach you about medicine. A doctor uses product knowledge to do two things: first, to make a proper diagnosis — that is, discover the patient's needs. Second, to explain, justify, and defend (if necessary) the diagnosis when the patient has concerns or questions.

Product knowledge is important for a doctor. However, it only has value if the doctor knows how to use it properly.

It's the same in sales. Product knowledge is important for you to be able to understand your prospect's situation and make a proper diagnosis of their needs. Product knowledge is also important as you present your diagnosis and as you work to convince your prospects that they should take action to fill those needs.

Product Knowledge

Keep the following things in mind as you read and study in preparation to practice the skills required for you to be your best.

1. *Prospects do not need or want to understand everything they buy.* Each year, millions of people buy cars with fuel injection and yet, very few can explain what it is or what it does. In fact, most people don't even care what fuel injection is. They only care that the dealer knows and that the dealer can fix it if it breaks. The only time fuel injection should ever been mentioned is when there is a direct benefit that the prospect wants.

2. *Prospects do not buy your products for your reasons.* Your features and benefits mean nothing if the benefits have no value to the prospect. For instance, four-wheel drive is useless to my mother who refuses to drive off the road or in bad weather.

3. *Prospects don't even really want your product or service in most cases.* Millions of drills are sold each year, not because people want a drill, but because they want a hole in something. Billions of dollars are spent each week in restaurants — not because people want to eat or even need to eat. Restaurants exist because people want and are willing to pay for one or a combination of the following: convenience, quality (some people can't cook), atmosphere, tax deduction, etc.

4. *Prospects don't always know what they want.* Nobody knew they wanted a computer until they knew what it could do, and they perceived a personal benefit. Computers have been around for years, and some people still don't know they want one because they don't perceive a benefit that outweighs the cost.

5. *Prospects don't generally want to know everything you know unless they are trying to replace you.* There are few things worse than a salesperson who drones on and on about their product or service instead of focusing on their prospect's needs.

6. *The more you talk about your products and services, the less the prospect will feel compelled to tell you about their needs.* If you tell them everything about your product or service, why would they need to tell you anything about their need?

7. *If you waste a prospect's time by talking too much about your products and services, they will be less likely to want to see you in the future.* Think of someone you like to avoid. Ask yourself why. Most likely, they waste your time and never bring you a benefit.

8. *Prospects do not typically recommend overly talkative salespeople to their business acquaintances or friends.* When was the last time you recommended an overly chatty salesperson to one of your friends? On the contrary, you will readily recommend "good listening" salespeople.

Having product knowledge is important. Using it correctly is critical. Using it poorly will destroy opportunities.

Where do you get it?

Assume responsibility for your own training. Don't assume your company will give you good training. If they do, that's great! Whether they do or don't, make a personal commitment to be the most knowledgeable person in your company. Study all available information: company literature, competitive literature, trade magazines, Internet home pages, the library, etc.

Ask questions. It's safe and expected that you will ask questions when you are new. Take advantage of this honeymoon period when asking questions. It's a sign of aggressiveness and diligence . . . not a sign of ignorance.

It is also to your advantage to identify a mentor, if possible. This should be a person in your company or industry who already is knowledgeable and successful. A mentor can help you save time by helping you to understand the products and services as well as the features and benefits that are attractive to your typical prospects and customers.

Give your prospects and customers the perception that you are an expert by really being an expert!

Fortunately, anyone who is willing to study can become expert enough to sell proficiently within a very short time.

Product knowledge can help you to improve your sales technique in three ways:

First, it can help you to construct questions so you can probe and learn your prospect's real needs. The questions you ask in a sales call should be designed to uncover current methods, problems, solutions, etc., which can be enhanced or fixed with your products and services.

Second, product knowledge can help you to differentiate your products and services from your prospect's alternative choices. This is critical because people make decisions based on the differences between alternative products and services.

Third, product knowledge will help you to understand your prospect's answers to your probing, so you can match your products and services to their real needs. You must know the benefits that your products and services provide so you can help your prospect see and understand them.

Product knowledge is important for all of the above-listed reasons, but again, it will not make the sale for you.

A good guideline is to always talk *less* than 50% of the time. Ask questions and encourage your prospects to talk. If you want to understand their need, you have to eventually let them talk anyway! Sooner is better than later!

The right amount of talking during a sales call is almost always less than you think! One of the most obnoxious characteristics of the "Webster Salesperson" is too much talking, and not enough listening!

The amount of product knowledge required to sell for some companies is daunting. However, I have good news for you. (This next *Natural Selling Concept* is one of the best-kept secrets in grade school, high school, and college.)

NATURAL SELLING CONCEPT #11

Life is an open book test. Selling is also an open book test. It is much better having product specification sheets, notes, samples, testimonials, etc., and not needing them, than not having them and wishing you did.

In today's world, prospects want salespeople who have the answers to all of their questions. They want to work with the experts. You don't want to have to tell a prospect that you are missing essential information. Some salespeople foolishly brag about "not having all the answers but knowing where to get them," as though false humility will impress their prospect. In sales, it is *never* impressive to say, "I don't know."

Decide now to have the necessary knowledge and decide now to be the expert. Decide now to be your best!

CHAPTER SEVEN
Finding / Developing the Real Need

Earlier, I defined selling as finding someone who has a need that your product or service can satisfy, and then filling that need in such a way that you both make a profit or gain.

Finding or developing *real needs* is the crux of our definition.

People call needs by different names: problems, opportunities, pain, buying motives, hotspots, goals, and many others. It makes no difference what words you use as long as you recognize them as needs and, more importantly, as long as your prospect recognizes them as needs!

Sometimes prospects have needs that everyone knows about; you, the prospect, the competition . . . everyone is already aware, and the need is fairly well defined.

Other times, prospects may not be aware of their problems or the opportunities and solutions that are available. Abraham Lincoln and John F. Kennedy did not know that they needed tighter security, and tighter security would have easily been available if the need had been known. Unknown needs can be just as valid and critical as known needs.

Part of your job is to help prospects see all of their needs — known and unknown — and then help them to realize that taking positive action will bring them more benefit than cost.

NATURAL SELLING CONCEPT #12

The only reason anyone buys anything is the perception that the total benefit they will receive is greater than the total cost they will incur.

You can learn a lot about identifying needs from medical professionals.

Medical people must quickly and accurately identify your needs, and sometimes you may not even know you have them. You might be totally aware, like when a bone is sticking out. On the other hand, you might only have symptoms, for instance, a pain in your stomach. But sometimes you have no known symptoms or problems, and a shadow shows up on an x-ray that takes you by total surprise.

Selling is very similar. Sometimes prospects know what they want. Sometimes they recognize their need, but aren't sure how *best* to fill it. And, sometimes they aren't even aware that they have a need.

Consider the following medical scenario that illustrates how most salespeople currently approach prospects.

Let's say you are out of town and you injure your shoulder. You go to a nearby clinic. Holding your shoulder in pain, you approach the nurse on duty.

She says, "What seems to be the problem?"

You say, "I have a sore shoulder."

She writes, "Sore shoulder" on her clipboard.

Then she says, "Let me get a little information and see if one of our doctors can have a look." This is nurse-talk for, "If you have a way to pay, the doctor might have a way to help — if you do not have a way to pay, then you are still going to have a sore shoulder."

Finding / Developing the Real Need

You show her an insurance card, and she shows you into a small furnished room with a paper-covered half-bed, sink, chair and mirror.

Eventually, a doctor walks in carrying the clipboard.

His nametag says, "Dr. Webster."

You think, "Hmmm!"

He says, "Before we get started, let me tell you a little about our medical practice. We have been in business eighteen years and we have seven doctors on staff. We have over one hundred fifty years of combined medical experience and we have twelve nurses. That's over one and a half nurses per doctor, which is an excellent ratio. Each doctor specializes in different areas, and my specialty is hemorrhoids. Last year I personally did over one hundred hemorrhoidectomies and didn't lose a single patient. Even though you may not currently have problems in that area, there's a good chance you will at some point in your life, so I would like to give you a brief overview of our capabilities. In fact, I have some literature I would like to give you that shows some of the problems that can develop if hemorrhoids are not treated properly. Perhaps, we might even do a quick examination to see if you are a candidate for one of our high-quality surgeries. However, before we proceed, do you have any questions?"

You say, "Only one question — are there any other doctors available?"

As silly as this scenario sounds, that is the way most salespeople sell. They think selling is telling a prospect all about their products and services and then giving out literature. Dr. Webster, in this example, typifies the Webster approach to selling, the wrong approach!

If you were a carpenter, you wouldn't say, "Before you tell me what you want me to build, let me tell you about the quality and composition of my screwdriver." The truth is, customers don't care about your screwdriver unless they have a screw loose — pun intended.

Now, suppose in the sore shoulder illustration, that Dr. Webster left and Dr. Natural came in with the same clipboard. He looks to be about a hundred years old but very healthy and alert. He sits down and asks, "What seems to be the problem?"

Interesting question! Even though this guy looks like he has seventy-five years of experience, and he has a clipboard with "sore shoulder" clearly written in the "problem" block — even though he has probably treated thousands of sore shoulders, you don't get upset when he asks, "What seems to be the problem?"

Why not? Because he is talking about you! Not about himself.

You answer, "I have a sore shoulder."

"Which shoulder?"

"My right shoulder."

He says, "Sharp pain or dull pain?"

"Sharp."

"What were you doing when it happened?"

You say, "Carrying a heavy sample case."

"Have you seen another doctor about this?"

You say, "I don't think so." (Dr. Webster is still fresh in your mind.)

"Have you tried any over-the-counter remedies?"

"No."

"Has anyone taken an x-ray?"

"No."

"Let's get one right now (closing the first sale), and then we will know the best way to treat the problem." (He's getting set up for the second sale.)

You say, "Sounds good!"

Dr. Webster's credibility and your confidence in him were both destroyed by his trying to sell himself. Dr. Natural established credibility and built your confidence by asking questions about you and listening to your answers.

If Dr. Natural asks good questions and has good answers to your questions, he may sell you on allowing him to put a knife into your shoulder on his way to fixing your problem.

You think you have a tough sell, try convincing someone to allow you to put a knife into their shoulder!

Yet, you will allow a doctor to do it, but not on the strength of his telling you about himself or because of how well he educated you, and certainly not because he has beautiful hemorrhoid brochures. You will allow it based on the confidence you gained by the intelligence and pertinence of his questions and his subsequent answers to yours.

In summary, doctors use product knowledge for two primary reasons. First, to know the questions to ask so they can make a proper diagnosis (identify the patient's needs) and suggest the best (there's only one best) treatment. Second, they use product knowledge to explain, justify, and defend (if necessary) the diagnosis when the patient has concerns or questions.

Your job, as it relates to product knowledge, is basically the same.

How do you identify your prospect's needs?

You actually started identifying needs in the prospecting (research) step, and then you continued in the first-contact step.

Assuming you have researched accurately and gathered some additional information when setting your appointment (whether it will be on the phone or in person), then you are ready for the next step.

That next step is communicating!

It has been said that 80% of the world's problems are caused by poor communication and the other 20% are probably caused by good communication. Since communication is so critical, let's look at some of the principles that govern it.

What communication principles should you keep in mind when selling?

1. *All forms of communication are some form of sales technique.* Every communication has a purpose. That purpose is always to influence somebody else's thinking, feeling or doing.

    "Influencing" means you are impacting someone's decision-making process. Our first *Natural Selling Concept* said, "Selling is getting someone to make a decision that they would not make if you weren't there." Therefore, all forms of communication are some form of sales technique.

2. *Most people believe that they are logical thinkers. However, their thoughts are influenced by feelings that are not always logical.* Therefore, people also speak in a way that is not always logical. However, they do not normally recognize the lack of logic, nor are they likely to agree that this is true. If you want to communicate effectively, you must understand your prospect's logic, as they see it. This is called their perspective. The best way to learn the other person's perspective —

to understand their filter system *(Figure 1-1)* — is to listen to that person. The *best* way to get into a listening mode is by asking questions.

3. *When you push a person, their natural response will be to resist and to push back.*

Try this exercise: Ask someone (a family member or someone who knows you) to hold their right hand up with their palm out in a gesture that looks like they are saying "HALT!" Now, facing that person, take your right hand (without telling what you are doing) and place your palm in opposition to theirs. Then gently start to push their hand, slowly increasing the pressure. There is a 95% likelihood that they will stiffen their arm and hand and start pushing back.

Ask, "Why are you pushing me?" They will probably say, "Because you pushed me," or, "Because I didn't want you to fall over," or they might even say, "I don't know!"

The real reason they almost always push back is because pushing back is a lamb. It's the most appropriate and most natural thing to do when pushed. It's a habit pattern! When you are selling, if you do not want the buyer to push back, you must listen and demonstrate that you understand their real needs.

When you tell somebody something, you are pushing their thinking. It is a natural reflex (a lamb) to push back. Not only will listening help you understand your customer's filter system, it's also the best way not to push your customer. The best way to get into a listening mode is — you guessed it — ask questions.

Natural Selling Concepts

4. *You never learn anything when you're talking.* You might learn a little by watching body language, but that's easy to misinterpret! The *best* way to learn about their goals, feelings, desires — *their needs* — is to be listening and the *best* way to get into a listening mode is to ask questions. (Starting to sound a little repetitive, isn't it?)

5. *The best way to confirm understanding is to paraphrase.* You paraphrase when you restate the other person's communication using *different words* in the form of a question: <u>"So what you're saying is . . ."</u> You will be amazed how many times your prospect will respond with, "No, that's not what I meant; what I meant was . . ."

   Paraphrasing helps you to communicate more accurately because it forces your prospect to repeat what they are saying, and it forces you to listen because you just asked a question.

6. *The person who is asking the best questions will most effectively guide or influence the direction of the sales call.* When you ask a question, in effect, you are deciding the subject (and direction) of conversation.

   One of the characteristics of human beings is that we do not like being told what to do. That started in the Garden of Eden, and human beings have had conflict ever since. Telling someone something is like pushing the conversation in a certain direction.

   Asking a question, however, is more like encouraging the other person to push. Then you have the option to agree or push back. If you want to control the direction of the conversation, you must use questions and then decide if, when, and how to push back. If your questions are safe — not personal or confidential in nature — there is a good possibility that you will move the conversation in the direction that your questions point, which coincidentally just happens to be in the direction of using your products or services.

Another good reason to ask more than you tell: People like giving answers to questions. Assuming your questions are relevant and intelligent, you will make your prospect feel good. It's probably a conditioned response that started in kindergarten when you were rewarded for having answers and then reinforced for the next twelve to twenty years of formal education.

Additionally, you build relationships quicker with people when you ask questions. Questions give your prospects "worth" and "personal value" by physically demonstrating that you respect their expertise.

One side benefit for you is that the prospect is never wrong when answering.

7. *It's a valuable skill to be able to answer a question and immediately come back with your own question without being obnoxious.* Some salespeople have been taught to answer every question from a prospect with an immediate question of their own. Answering a question with a question can be good if asked in the right way. However, it can come across very "Websterish" (obnoxious) if you are not careful. When your prospect says, "What does it cost?" you do not want to answer, "How much do you think it costs?" or "How much would you like it to cost?" Those answers border on being rude.

It is much better to just answer your prospect's questions and then come back with a question of your own. You could easily say, "That service (or product) is normally in the $2,000 to $10,000 range, but let me ask you a couple of questions, and then I can give you a more exact figure."

Answering questions and then immediately coming back with your own question is valuable because it allows you to continue to guide the direction of conversation — the direction of the sales call. This is critical to identifying needs because whenever prospects ask you questions, they are also hinting at their needs. You must come back with a question or you may lose the opportunity to discover those needs.

For example, suppose your prospect just asked how long your company has been in business. Ask yourself, "Do they really care how many years we have been around?" The answer is an obvious, no! They've asked about how long your company has been around because they may want to do business with a well-established company with a long track record of success and of paying their bills. On the other hand, they might want a company that's new and innovative; one that is not stuck in the past with heavy overhead costs. The painful truth is that when a prospect asks how long your company has been in business, you really don't know why they asked. Hence, they are hinting that you should — you must — follow with a question to clarify their real need.

Your best answer might sound something like: "We have actually been in business x years. We're well established, and yet we're very flexible. What characteristics are you looking for in a supplier?"

Remember, at this point, you are trying to identify your prospect's needs. Later, in the presentation, you will show how your experience, innovation, etc., meet those needs.

8. *If you want to sell what your buyer buys, then you must look through your buyer's eyes.* People buy for their own reasons, not yours.

   If you could know everything about your prospect — likes, dislikes, feelings, thoughts, prejudices, desires, goals, dreams, heartaches, past experiences, pains, and all of those other things that make each prospect unique — if you could know those things, you could easily decide if your product or service could fill their needs. In addition, you would have the information you need to be able to start matching your products and services to those needs. In fact, more and more companies today acquire just this type of information to qualify their prospects before any personal interaction occurs. But, at some point, person-to-person interaction is required, and asking questions and listening to your prospect can never be replaced by automated data collecting.

   The best way to learn about your prospect is to listen — and the best way to get into a listening mode is to ask questions.

9. *Over 4,000 years ago, Solomon wrote, "Even a fool is thought wise if he remains silent, and discerning if he holds his tongue." It was true then; it's still true today!* . . . Quiet people tend to look more intelligent than talkative people. Since they have more time for listening, they even have the opportunity to be more intelligent.

Natural Selling Concepts

Principles don't change! The best way to look intelligent is to speak less than the prospect. The best way to hold your tongue is to be listening, and the best way to get into a listening mode is to ask questions.

What do you need to remember from these communication principles?

1) The purpose of communicating is to influence — to sell.

2) Since people think in illogical ways and do not like being told what to do, you will be more successful if you ask questions and then listen to the answers.

3) Speaking words doesn't mean you are communicating. Paraphrase the other person's comments and verify that you are both on the same page.

4) Questions guide the direction of the communication. Use questions often. Whenever your prospect asks you a question, answer it and then ask them a question right away to see what "hint" they might have been giving.

5) Try to look at their needs through their eyes and encourage them to talk more than you. You will learn more, and they will think you are smarter than you might really be.

This is the time in our seminars where we ask attendees to tell us what the most important award-winning skill is in selling. Ninety-nine percent of the time, the response is "listening!"

Good answer, but wrong!

The correct answer is that the most important award-winning skill in selling is *asking questions.* Listening is important as well, but it is more important that you are listening to the *right* information.

Asking the right questions helps you to listen and learn real needs.

Natural Selling Concept #13
Telling ain't selling — Asking is!
(Listening ain't selling either!)

You would think that a skill as important as asking questions would be taught in high schools, colleges and universities, but it's not! In fact, over 90% of *Fortune 500* CEOs have direct selling experience and yet, not one of them has a college degree in sales or selling and, to my knowledge, none have ever had a course in questioning prospects or listening. That's because colleges and universities do not offer degrees in sales or selling. Moreover, they don't even offer courses in asking questions and listening. That's 90% of the top people in the top publicly owned companies in America who have needed and used skills that are not emphasized in any school in the world.

How do you improve your ability to ask questions?
1st — *List all of the titles of people who currently buy your products and services:* accountants, administrative assistants, buyers, CEOs, company owners, government officials, home owners, human resources managers, manufacturing managers, marketing managers, operations managers, parents, plant managers, presidents, purchasing agents, sales managers, secretaries, VPs, etc.

Natural Selling Concepts

All prospects tend to fit into one of the following categories:

- **Economic:** Primary interests will be in cost, terms, budget, delivery, etc. Their needs tend to relate to dollars.
- **Technical:** Primary interests will be in function. (Will your "solution" be the best?) Their needs tend to relate to quality.
- **User:** Primary interests will be in ease of implementation or use. Their needs tend to relate to personal goals.
- **Owner:** Primary interests will be in ROI (return on investment) — company image. Their needs tend to relate to stockholder response and corporate goals.

You can list as many titles as you want, but you will probably cover 90% of your prospects if you focus on the top three to five.

2nd — Develop a "Top-10" list of best questions for each of these titles.

The task may seem daunting, but once you start, you will see that there really are only thirty to fifty good questions for each title. Brainstorm to develop a good list and then, narrow it down to the ten best for each title.

Many of these best questions will appear on every list, and that's okay! Expect your questions to be 60% to 70% the same on each list.

For example, each of your lists might contain the following questions along with your own industry-product- or service-specific questions.

1. "Are you familiar with our company (our new service or product)?"
2. "How are you currently generating the benefits that our products or services generate?" [Use your own words here.]
3. "How did you get started in this business?"
4. "When it comes to making decisions in this area, do you normally make them on your own, or do you consult with others?"
5. "What benefit would you gain by moving forward with . . ? What might you lose if you don't move forward with . . ?"
6. "How soon would you like to have this completed?"
7. Industry or product-specific question . . .
8. Et cetera.

Make your lists using these questions or any of your own; as long as you are convinced that your "Top-10" list is the best.

The following examples are provided to help you develop your lists.

PRODUCT & SERVICE

"How are you currently generating the benefits that (our products or services) generate?" *[Use your own words.]*

"If you had an extra $100,000, what would you improve in the _____ area?"

BUDGET & ACCOUNTING

"Do you have money set aside already?"

"If we can show a significant return on investment, could you 'find' the money?"

"Are you open to leasing or financing?"

"Would it be okay for me to contact someone in your accounting department to set up an account for you?"

"How do you currently make budgeting decisions? Is it based on the time to pay back the original investment?"

TIMING OR URGENCY

"How did this (project, objective, etc.) get started?"

"What might you gain if you made a decision to go forward?"

"What might you lose if you do not go forward?"

"How soon would you like to have this in place? . . . Complete? . . . Resolved?"

DECISION-MAKERS AND INFLUENCERS

Note: There are literally millions of ways to ask a person if they are the real decision-maker. Unfortunately, most of these questions do not generate a completely accurate answer. If you ask my wife *or* me, "Are you the final decision-maker when it comes to buying furniture?" . . . We will *both* answer, "Yes." And . . . we will both be telling the truth! We are both final decision-makers because we can both say, "No!" There really are millions of ways to ask who the real decision-maker is — but how many best ways are there? Only one! The best I have ever heard is:

"Mr. _____, when it comes to making decisions concerning _____, do you normally make final decisions on your own, or do you discuss them with other people?"

COMPETITIVE ENVIRONMENT — PROSPECT'S ALTERNATIVES

"What alternatives have you considered, if any?"

PROSPECT'S "TOTAL" NEED

"If this works well, what will you do next?"

"Can you tell me a little about your company growth plans?"

PROSPECT'S CONFIDENCE LEVEL IN YOU AND YOUR COMPANY

"Have you worked with our company before?"

"Are you familiar with our history as a company?"

PROSPECT'S CURRENT PREFERENCES

"What are your most critical preferences?" (Lowest cost? Quality? Safety? Delivery?)

3rd — *Practice! Practice! Practice! "Smooth" and "effective" are characteristics you will develop over time.*
The more you practice, the smoother (more natural) you become. The smoother you become, the more effective you can become. Practice is the key.

4th — *Constantly look for better "Top-10" questions.*
Only replace a question with one that's better. That way, your list will always be best.

Natural Selling Concepts

5th — *Practice when you are not selling!* See if you can carry on a conversation with questions. See how many questions you can ask before the other person notices.

You will know when you have been "caught" by watching the other person's eyes. When one eye half closes and the other eye opens wider — you have been caught. That's called "busted." See how many questions you can ask in a row without getting busted.

If you think you are a real natural, just try that exercise and see.

One other caution — practice with people who aren't chatterboxes. Some people talk so much they make you nervous. They never use a sentence if they have a paragraph available. You can ask these people fifty questions in a row and they will never suspect what you are doing. Practice on people who are quieter — people who tend to be more introverted and more into listening than expressing their own views. Even though it is more difficult to carry on conversations with quiet people, you will learn more and your question-asking skill will grow significantly.

One additional word of caution: Your objective is to get better at asking questions naturally so you can also get better at understanding the other person's perspective and needs. Asking questions is a learned skill and learned skills must be practiced.

Three of the best places to practice are with waiters/waitresses, with family and with friends.

Waiters and waitresses are paid to ask questions and record information. If you try to "out ask" them, they will go along. They will *not* get upset or *even notice* if you do it smoothly.

One time I ordered a meal with questions only and

nobody even suspected I was practicing. I had decided on chicken cordon bleu and the following "conversation" took place:

Waiter:	"Are you ready to order?"
Me:	"What do you recommend?"
Waiter:	"Our steaks are our specialty."
Me:	"How's your chicken?"
Waiter:	"Our chicken Kiev is excellent."
Me:	"What about your chicken cordon bleu?"
Waiter:	"It's also very good."
Me:	"Can I go with the chicken cordon bleu?"
Waiter:	"Sure! Would you like a salad?"
Me:	"What's the house dressing?"
Waiter:	. . . Answers . . .
Me:	. . . Another question . . .

Try to order lunch or dinner with questions only. It's easy if you practice. Watch the other person's expression and see if you can avoid being busted. The first time you try this, it will probably be a bit uncomfortable. That is not a bad sign! It means you are not as natural as you think. It means you need to practice.

Another time, I tried the exercise with my wife. I figured I was pretty good at conversing with questions, but a funny thing happened. On my third question, she stopped reading her book, looked up at me with one eyebrow up and the other down and said, "Why do you suddenly care?"

Busted on my third question.

The nice part about practicing this skill is that you can do it with anyone and the other person doesn't even have to know. In fact, through the years I have been able to get as high as nine questions with Pam, my wife, before she looks at me and says, "Oh, you're playing that silly game again, aren't you?"

My response, "Well, yeah, but you didn't really notice at first did you?" (In case you missed it, that was question number ten.)

Practice asking questions when you are not selling and you will be a better question-asker when you are. If you do not practice, it will not make you worse, but you cannot be your best if you do not practice.

Summary

You can only sell at your best when you understand the other person's needs, and then most appropriately position or adjust your offering to fill those needs. Position is an advertising term that refers to what you do to cause your prospect to have a desired perception of your product or service.

To illustrate, consider the following example: If you are a manufacturer of grape jelly, you will position and sell your product to a consumer differently than you would to large restaurant chains. To the consumer, you might stress taste and nutrition. To the large restaurant chain, you might stress that consumers like it, and it's very cost-effective when you purchase it in bulk by the railroad-tanker load.

To the large restaurant chain that is concerned about image, you might even suggest they repackage it in classic containers and re-sell it under their own name.

Each customer has different needs.

Your challenge is to understand those needs (as they relate to your products or services) better than your prospect. You can only do this through questioning and then listening.

Once you have identified needs that you and your company can satisfy, you are ready to qualify those needs; you are ready to make sure that the prospect is still in the boat with you. You are ready to go on to the next step — the Up-Front Contract.

CHAPTER EIGHT

Qualifying Needs and Decision-Makers and Closing Early
(also known as "Up-Front Contracts")

Wouldn't it be great if prospective buyers never objected? Wouldn't it be great if they never said, "Your price is too high," or "I want to think it over," or "I'm already working with your competitor?"

There is a popular myth in selling that objections are not bad because "They are the prospect's way of telling you what's most important." Unfortunately, this is not true. It is much easier to learn what is important to a prospect by asking good questions and listening carefully. Objections are really the prospect's way of saying, "You haven't really qualified me yet; we're going to slow down now, and if you don't have a really good reason to continue, you are going to lose my business."

Fortunately, there is an easier and much safer way to qualify prospects and discover what is important to them. It's called the "Up-Front Contract," or the UFC.

The Up-Front Contract is a verbal agreement between a buyer and a seller to move forward when certain conditions are met.

A basic UFC says, "If I do something, will you respond in a certain way?" "If our company can meet your need, will you give us the order?" "If our price is reasonable, will you help me to set up a meeting with your CEO?"

The format is always: *"If I do A, will you do B?"*

Consider the following examples:

Natural Selling Concepts

1. "If we provide you with samples, will you test them?"
2. "If these samples test good, will you specify them on your engineering drawing?"
3. "Would you be willing to give me a trial order if we can meet your delivery requirement?"
4. "If we can do the job, can we have the order?"

The UFC gets its name from its timing in the sales process. It is used "up front" before you start your presentation. It is used as soon as possible after you identify your prospect's real need and before you start presenting how your product or service will fill the need. *(Ref: Fig 2.1)*

Up-Front Contracts do five things better than any other tool in the salesperson's bag:

1. UFCs qualify the real need.
2. UFCs qualify the real decision-maker(s).
3. UFCs identify the concerns that will surface later as objections if not properly handled.
4. UFCs save time. They help to insure the prospect is qualified, interested and willing to work with you before you actually present your product or service. Why invest the time and effort to prepare and present if the prospect is not qualified, interested, or willing to work with you?
5. UFCs are the quickest and safest way to start asking for the order before the presentation.

Remember our definition of selling: *Selling is finding a prospect with a need that your product or service can satisfy and then filling the need in such a way that you and your prospect both make a gain.* An agreed-upon Up-Front Contract is the best way to be sure you have identified and agreed upon one of your prospect's real needs.

Some people refer to Up-Front Contracts as Up-Front Closes, but be careful!

If closing an order is like getting married, then the Up-Front Contract (UFC) is more like getting engaged. It is not necessarily a close or an irrevocable commitment. It is an agreement to make a commitment later, after you satisfy your half of the Up-Front Contract.

Between the Up-Front Contract (engagement) and the close (wedding) there may be much work to do.

Why would a couple invest time, effort and money in preparation and details if they had not pre-agreed to say, "I do," when the time comes for the close?

The Up-Front Contract serves the same purpose in business as the proposal in marriage: It is asking your prospect for an agreement to make a positive decision or commitment before you invest significant time, effort and money. You can spend hours, weeks or even longer doing the work necessary to close a sale. The UFC (early in the sales process) is the best way to make sure your efforts will be rewarded.

Having an Up-Front Contract is the most important prerequisite to starting your presentation. It helps to insure that you have a qualified prospect who has qualified needs.

Picture yourself arriving at a major sporting event after a long drive through heavy traffic. You park and walk what seems like two miles. You finally arrive at the gate and suddenly realize you left your tickets at home on the kitchen table.

The feeling in the pit of your stomach is the same feeling you get when trying to close (complete) a significant sale and suddenly discovering you are working with a non-decision-maker. Or perhaps you ask for a commitment only to discover there are two more proposals yet to be received.

Now, because of these surprise issues, you cannot close.

The purpose of the Up-Front Contract is to help you identify and deal with all of the critical issues before your presentation . . . before you are surprised.

NATURAL SELLING CONCEPT #14

Your best presentations are the ones you make to qualified prospects who have qualified needs, and who have said "yes" to your Up-Front Contract.

Certain critical issues must be addressed before you can make your best presentation. (These critical issues if addressed properly, help to insure that you have a qualified prospect with qualified needs.)

NATURAL SELLING CONCEPT #15

The critical issues that must be addressed before you can make your best (most effective) presentation are:

1. You must have a valid decision-maker who can move the process forward (toward a close).
2. You must know that your product or service will bring value to your prospect.
3. You must understand your prospect's decisioning process.
4. Your prospect must agree that there is a need.
5. Your prospect must agree that there is more value to be gained by going forward rather than waiting.

6. Your prospect must understand how they can fit your solution into their budget. (Keep in mind, your prospect can always fit your solution into their budget if the value they believe they will receive will be greater than the total cost they believe they will pay. Their total (perceived) cost involves more than price and financing charges. Their total real cost includes lost-opportunity costs. Lost-opportunity costs are those associated with not meeting alternative or conflicting needs. Every decision to invest in one area costs you the option to invest in another. When my wife agreed to get married, part of the cost to her was that the rest of the men of the world instantly became off limits.)

7. Your prospect must trust you enough to be willing to work with you (to allow you) to fill their need.

Once you have properly addressed these issues, you have a qualified prospect.

Any issue that has not been fully addressed before the presentation may become the objection that derails you after the presentation when you are trying to close.

The better you address these seven issues, the fewer objections you will run into later.

Now, here is the beautiful thing about UFCs.

When you ask for an Up-Front Contract, any response other than an unqualified yes is an early warning that you probably have not adequately addressed all seven issues.

It is typical to have clauses (additions and exceptions) in legal contracts. It is also typical to have clauses in UFCs.

Natural Selling Concepts

These verbal clauses are your prospect's way of telling you what issues will come up later as objections, if not addressed in the presentation.

For example, suppose you identified a need and your prospect expressed concern about your completion date.

You tried the following UFC.

"If we show you how we will complete the project ahead of your schedule, will you commit to giving us the go ahead today?"

Your prospect responded,

"It depends on the overtime charges."

At this point, you do not have an Up-Front Contract. Your prospect has revealed an additional issue related to price. In other words, they just hung a "clause" on your UFC and gave it back to you. Your response should be to add the clause and restate the UFC, "Then, you're saying, we can go ahead if we can meet your schedule and if our price is good?" If your prospect responds affirmatively, you have your UFC and can proceed to the presentation.

Consider another example:

Salesperson: "If this product meets your need, can we go ahead with an order today?"

Prospect: "It depends on the price and if I would have to pay for it right away." (Remember: You do NOT have an Up-Front Contract until your prospect says, "Yes!")

Salesperson: "Then, you're saying we can go ahead if the price is right and if we can agree on acceptable payment terms?" (The prospect had two questions or concerns about the contract. The salesperson recognized an incomplete UFC and offered a new UFC with two clauses.)

The prospect now has three options:

(a) say yes to the new contract with its two clauses,

(b) present a new question that would require another clause, or

(c) say no if he or she is not the decision-maker or if there is no real perceived need for the product or service.

The first two responses move you closer to an order — if an order is possible.

The third option saves you time by helping you quickly identify and address unresolved issues. For example, suppose the prospect answers,

"No we can't go forward because John will have to approve this, and John is out of town until Monday."

In other words, you just found out there is another decision-maker. Your best strategy now might be to change your Up-Front Contract to,

"Let's do this — let's look at our pricing and payment terms. Then, if they look good to you, would you be willing to set up a meeting with you, John and me on Monday when he gets back?"

The Up-Front Contract is an agreement that we have identified and agreed upon all of the known issues — and, that we are willing to move forward when those issues are handled or resolved. Up-Front Contracts are powerful when used by honest, ethical salespeople to speed up the sales process.

Unfortunately, they are also powerful when used by unscrupulous, unethical salespeople to take advantage of prospects. Webster salespeople use UFCs to manipulate prospects, and this is one of the reasons that the sales profession generally has a poor reputation.

Natural Selling Concepts

You have probably encountered this yourself!

If you have ever bought a car, there is about a 50% chance that you have been exposed to a Webster salesperson using (actually abusing) UFCs. It sounds something like this: "I'm not sure I can sell the car at that price. However, if you'll write me a check for $500 to show you're serious, I will take it to my manager to see if he will agree."

You know he already knows if he can accept the deal.

He knows you know that he knows if he can accept the deal.

Webster salespeople abuse the UFC when they say, "I'm not sure we can accept your offer, but . . ." when in fact, they know if they can! They are abusing the UFC by starting it with a lie, and everyone (prospect and salesperson) knows it's a lie. So, why do they do it?

There are two reasons.

First, they are taught by "Webster Managers" who have never been trained in honesty and ethics themselves. They know that if they can get you to write a check, you will mentally start taking possession of the product or service. They can now come back and negotiate you up several percentage points on price because they know you will not want to lose possession of your product or service on a relatively minor price difference.

Second, it works! It gets the average salesperson to ask for the order, and it gets the average prospect to make a decision. It gets your emotions involved. You are being deceived into believing that you are pushing the seller and getting a good deal. The technique gets you to stop thinking about the merits of the product or service and only think about possession. You will probably make a buying decision before you are really sold, often resulting in the feeling that you were pushed or manipulated.

The Webster approach is bad because it is built on a lie. Lying is never necessary!

Some sales managers and owners want new business so much that they are willing to rationalize away some of their integrity and honesty. Fortunately, many honest and ethical automobile salespeople use Up-Front Contracts with integrity.

Change the UFC to, "If we can put a deal together today that meets all of your needs, are you ready to make a decision?" and now you have a good Up-Front Contract. It accomplishes all of the good things you want, but without the manipulation.

Up-Front Contracts can be soft or hard.

The less sure you are that the prospect is ready to move forward — the softer you will want the UFC to be.

Examples of soft UFCs:

"Mr. Smith, if we can assure delivery by Friday, will that help you to decide?"

"If we could show you a way to save 15% in labor, would you be interested?"

"Assuming we have the best overall proposal, would you consider working with us?"

"If we find a solution that works, will you want to move forward quickly?"

Examples of hard UFCs:

"Mr. Smith, if we can assure delivery by Friday, will you give us the go ahead to start?"

"If we could show you a way to save 15% in labor, would you give us the contract?"

"Assuming we have the best overall proposal, will you give us the go ahead on the order today?"

"If we find a solution that works, do we have your approval to start?"

Read the next sentence twice! **The primary issues that need to be addressed in your presentation are those that are part of the Up-Front Contract.** You do not have to sell quality if your prospect is already sold on your quality or if your prospect is not concerned with quality. You do not have to sell price if your prospect is already sold on your price or if your prospect is not concerned with price.

You never have to do a full presentation unless your prospect objects about everything, and that is not likely to happen. Once you fulfill your half of the Up-Front Contract, you will have dealt with all of your prospect's objections during the presentation — before the close!

The whole goal of your presentation is to fulfill your end of the UFC and then ask for the order or commitment.

When you properly initiate an Up-Front Contract and get a yes, and then fulfill your half of the contract, you create a social obligation for your prospect to do his or her part as well.

It is not difficult to ask for and get Up-Front Contracts, but becoming skilled will take practice. It will probably be uncomfortable at first, but they become more comfortable as you gain experience using them. Just like any other important skill, it must be learned by preparation, trial and error and repetition!

Natural Selling Concept #16

The best way to avoid negative surprises when closing is to have a good Up-Front Contract.

Up-Front Contracts are extremely valuable. They save time and help you to know what you must cover in your presentation, which is the next step in the *Natural Selling Process*.

🦋 CHAPTER NINE 🦋

Presenting

People sometimes interchange the words <u>selling</u> and <u>presenting</u>. Selling is the whole process. Presenting is only a part of the process.

Presenting is the sixth part of the *Natural Selling Process (Figure 2-1)*. It comes after prospecting, making contact, establishing rapport, identifying real needs, and the Up-Front Contract.

<u>NATURAL SELLING CONCEPT #17</u>

The purpose of the presentation is to fill your half of the Up-Front Contract, which will generate a tacit or implied obligation on the part of your prospect to fill his or her half.

Presenting is not the beginning of the sale. It is actually the beginning of the close. You start your presentation after securing an Up-Front Contract. This means you have identified and qualified at least one need, you have identified and qualified the decision-making process and the decision-maker(s), and your prospect has agreed to go forward if you meet your "Up-Front" conditions.

For example, suppose you are selling accounting services, and your job is to sell companies on outsourcing their accounting needs. In other words, you are selling people on paying an outside company for their accounting needs instead of hiring their own employees.

You make a sales call on a small manufacturer and find out that they would like to lower their administrative costs.

You use your product knowledge to ask questions until you build an accurate understanding of their situation. You become convinced that if the prospect outsources their accounting function to your company it will lower their administrative costs and simultaneously generate a reasonable profit for your company.

You give the following Up-Front Contract:

"John, based on what I now know about your situation, I believe we could lower your administrative costs significantly if you would outsource your accounting functions to our company. If I could show you how we would do that for you, would you be in a position to give us the 'go-ahead' today?"

John (the decision-maker) says,

"Yes, assuming you can have the implementation completed by the first of next month."

You now have an Up-Front Contract with an additional "clause."

John has agreed to say yes . . . if you can show how his administrative costs would go down and . . . if you can complete the transition by the first of next month.

As soon as you fill your half of the Up-Front Contract, John will incur an obligation to fill his half of the Up-Front Contract. He will incur an obligation to give you the "go-ahead" today. Decision-makers like John do not have to keep their word, but an amazingly high percentage will!

Essentially, the Up-Front Contract tells you what you have to address in the presentation. Clauses to Up-Front Contracts are additional conditions that must also be met.

If you know all of the possible conditions and clauses, you can then develop all of the best "lambs" and "elevator speeches" *(Ref. Chapter 4)* that you will ever need.

NATURAL SELLING CONCEPT #18

You are prepared to make your presentation when you have *lambs* and *elevator speeches* available to address all of your prospect's Up-Front Contract conditions and clauses.

How many Up-Front Contract conditions and clauses are there?

You might think there are an infinite number of conditions and clauses, but there are remarkably few. In fact, all of your prospect's Up-Front Contract conditions and clauses can be addressed in the presentation if you are prepared to answer the following ten questions.

The first four questions only need to be answered if you are making a new contact.

1. Can you identify yourself? (Who are you? Where are you located?)

Remember from Chapter 5 (Establishing Rapport and Building Relationships) that people buy from people they like and trust. The first step in liking or trusting someone is knowing who they are.

Several years ago, while traveling with a relatively new salesperson, we made a sales call on a major prospect. The salesperson had secured an appointment and then made proper introductions when we arrived. We talked with the prospect for approximately twenty minutes and identified several small needs and one that was significant. The salesperson asked for and was granted an Up-Front Contract agreeing that we could have the order if we could meet the delivery requirements.

Natural Selling Concepts

The salesperson made a short telephone call, confirmed that the delivery requirements would be met and then asked for a purchase order. The prospect agreed. However, when he stood up to go have the purchase order typed, he turned and looked at the salesman and said, "You are with ABC Company, aren't you?" (ABC Company was the salesperson's competitor!)

The prospect was not joking! He had honestly not understood clearly who we were! Fortunately, he was not very familiar with ABC Company either.

The salesperson was embarrassed; I was embarrassed, and . . . the prospect was embarrassed! We were still given the order, but it is frightening to realize that prospects don't always know or remember you or your company's name.

I used to tell people that it didn't make much difference whether you gave a prospect your business card early in the sales call or at the end. I no longer believe that. It is important for them to know who you are and to remember who you are. One of the best ways to remind them is to have your card immediately available all through that first meeting. If your visits are infrequent, it might be good to present your card at the beginning of your second and third meetings as well.

2. What do you do? Many salespeople make the critical mistake of assuming they are communicating because they are speaking the same language as their prospect. I'm talking about salespeople who are speaking English to prospects who understand English, but who are not communicating because they are using words or jargon that are not familiar to their prospects.

One company that I worked with used to tell their prospects that they were a "large-roll specialty paper converter."

Based on these words, do you know what they do? Probably not!

This is an accurate description of what they do, but it does not communicate clearly to the average person.

It has been said, if you want to be understood by 90% of your audience, you should communicate at the seventh-grade level. If you try to impress your audience or prospect with sophisticated or technical language, you will likely miscommunicate, which impresses no one!

Once the large-roll specialty paper converter removed the jargon and explained what they did using seventh-grade words, they communicated more accurately. Now they say, "You know those small rolls of paper in cash registers . . . the ones that your receipt is printed on . . . well, we manufacture those rolls of paper."

Decide how you will describe what you sell and then test your description by telling someone who is not in your business. Then ask them to paraphrase what you said and see how accurately you communicated. Remember, there is only one best way to describe what you do. Make sure you know it and use it.

There is no reward for using confusing jargon or ten-syllable words. There are only rewards for accurate and clear communicating.

3. How are you different? (What separates you from other people in your business?)

Whenever a prospect can choose between you and your competitor, the decision will be made on your *differences*. Your strengths determine your competitor's weaknesses. Your weaknesses determine their strengths.

It is critical to your success that you distinguish how you are different from your competition and how you are able to provide better solutions to your prospect's needs.

You need to know who your competitors are and how you are stronger as well as how you are weaker. Be honest with yourself. This knowledge will help you to position yourself as the better choice by emphasizing your positives and minimizing your negatives.

4. Are you credible? (Whom have you worked with in the past? How long have you been in business?)

When prospects consider working with you, they will want assurances that you are who you say you are, and that you will do what you say you will do.

Every salesperson who has ever called on me has claimed to be high quality, among the best (if not the best), trustworthy, dependable, full of integrity, etc.

I have yet to hear one say, "You really should work with us . . . we're above average in some things and below in others."

It has been said that a résumé is a balance sheet with all assets and no liabilities. Salespeople tend to be a walking resume for their company, so prospects will want to check you out . . . assuming, that is, that they are considering working with you.

You need to be ready with testimonials, client lists, referrals, and any other documentation that verifies your credibility.

Testimonials are especially valuable. They are literally worth more than their weight in gold. Testimonials can do two things that you cannot do.

First, they can brag about you and your company and your products. You cannot brag because it would be self-serving and obnoxious. I heard it said once that conceit is the only disease that makes everyone sick except the person who has it.

Second, testimonials can put your competition down, but you cannot. Now listen carefully! You must *never* put your competition down, because putting them down would also be putting your prospect down. After all, the prospect has already said they are somewhat impressed or they wouldn't even be considering the competitor. To put a competitor down is like saying to the prospect, "You would have to be dumb as a box of rocks to work with those people, wouldn't you?" Chances are that your prospect will not appreciate that approach.

Now, think of the impact that you can have if you have a testimonial from someone who likes you and your company (products and services) better than your competitor. What do you think your prospect will say if you say the following,

> "Before you consider using anyone else, here's a testimonial letter from John Smith. Before you decide, call John. Ask him the difference between (competitor) and us. He's worked with both of us. Ask him the difference."

This is a powerful approach and in most cases, the prospect will not even call, because they already know what John is going to say. You made your point without directly putting your competitor (and prospect) down.

NOTE: The purpose of the previous two chapters was to identify and qualify needs. It was to help you "know" your prospect at a deeper level. It was to help make sure you would be able to answer questions 5, 6 and 7.

5. Do you have an understanding of my real need(s)?
It is not enough to know what your prospect needs. Your prospect must know that you know . . . and agree.

The purpose of the two prior steps in the *Natural*

Natural Selling Concepts

Selling Process (finding the real need and the Up-Front Contract) is to accomplish just that. If you have done those steps, then your prospect has agreed that you have an understanding of their real need and you are ready to proceed.

6. Do you understand my "filter system" (my value system and my goals)? Do you understand how I make decisions? What motivates me to make decisions the way I do?

Every decision-maker has a value system and each has been uniquely programmed. Your value system is the filter in your brain that converts sensory input data (what you hear, see, touch, taste and smell) into output actions or decisions. Your filter is made up of all of the data that you have stored since you were born. It consists of facts, feelings, and opinions . . . and everything else you have ever been exposed to. It even includes your thoughts on what you have been exposed to.

This programming defines your value system. Your value system defines your "common sense." Your common sense defines how you make decisions and what actions you will take as a response to the sensory input.

If you were raised in a family populated by staunch Democrats, you are very likely a Democrat. In a presidential debate, your common sense will tell you, "There's no question, the Democratic candidate's position was best." If you were raised in a family populated by staunch Republicans, there's a strong likelihood that you are a Republican. In the same presidential debate, your common sense will tell you, "There's no question, the Republican candidate's position was best." Once your programming has taken root, you will tend to believe your political perspective is the most common sense, logical and therefore, the best perspective.

Presenting

It is critically important to understand that you make decisions based more on your programming (your filter or value system) than on facts or reality. You make decisions based on how your programming allows you to interpret the facts. Your prospects will also make decisions based on their filter systems . . . Not based on facts and certainly not based on your filter system!

Suppose for example that you call on two different prospects, and you are selling computer hardware and services. You can sell individual things like monitors, keyboards, cables, software upgrades, etc., or complete systems including all hardware, software, installation, service contracts and ongoing maintenance. You can sell specific parts or you can sell a whole (turnkey) system.

However, before you attempt to sell either of these prospects, it is important to understand each prospect's value (filter) system.

Assume Prospect A and Prospect B are both forty years old and each manages twenty-five people. Within their respective companies, each is considered a rising star. They both graduated from college ten years earlier where each had worked on several project teams.

Prospect A did not have the sharpest team members and quickly learned that if you want something done right, you . . . *(You already know the answer because you have it programmed into your subconscious . . . your filter system!)* . . . If you want something done right, you need to do it yourself.

Prospect B did have sharp team members and quickly learned that if you want something done right, you need to plan, delegate and work through other people.

Prospect A and B each have managers who are very happy with their work. Prospect A's manager especially appreciates A's attention to details. However, A's manager does wish Prospect A was better at delegating.

Prospect B's manager especially appreciates B's ability to delegate. However, B's manager does wish Prospect B was better at details.

Now . . . you call on each of these prospects selling computer hardware and services.

If you attempt to sell a turnkey solution to each of these prospects, Prospect A will look at you with one eye half closed and think, "Yea, right! I've heard that before!" Then Prospect A will probably say something like,

> "That sounds interesting; why don't you leave some literature with me and I will give you a call."

Don't hold your breath waiting for the call!

However, Prospect B will look at you and think,

> "Okay! It's about time someone understood how to get things done."

Then B will say something like,

> "Let's sit down and talk about how we can get this thing going."

Now, consider a slightly different scenario.

You attempt to sell individual products and services to each of these prospects. You say,

> "We sell a number of different products and services and I would like to see which you might be interested in. We can then show you how to train your people and we can show you how to install everything, or we can install and train for you by working closely with you to get it done."

Prospect A will look at you and think, "Okay! It's about time someone understood the importance of details." Then, Prospect A will say something like,

> "Let's sit down and talk about how we can get this thing going."

Prospect B will look at you and think, "Yea, right! As if I don't have enough to do!" Then Prospect B will say something like,

"That sounds interesting; why don't you leave some literature with me and I will give you a call."

Don't hold your breath waiting for that call either!

You see, it's not **what you are selling** that really counts. It's **how what you are selling fits** through the prospect's filter system.

In these examples, if you understand your prospect's filter system (value system and goals), you can best position your products and services to fill the perceived needs in a way that makes most sense to your prospect!

7. Do you understand my/our decision-making process? The average U.S. company has 6.2 decision-makers because the average U.S. company has approximately 6.2 employees and each one can say, "No!" Everyone can say "No," but do you know who can say, "Yes," and do you know everyone who will be involved in the decisioning process?

Before you present your products or services, you should have identified and understood the decisioning process. If you haven't done that *(refer to Chapter 8)* and you are getting ready for your presentation, stop and find out. Making great presentations to people who cannot say yes can be a significant waste of time.

Every individual and every company has a decisioning process. Each is different.

So how do you make sure you understand?

Ask!

There are many ways to ask, but for your industry and your personality, there will only be one best.

Natural Selling Concepts

As you think through and construct *your* best way, consider the following:

1. (Poor) Are you the decision-maker?
2. (Okay) How do you make decisions like this?
3. (Best) When it comes to making decisions like this, do you normally make them alone or are there others you consult with first?

The third is best because it most effectively asks for a complete answer. Question #1 is like asking, "Are you important?" And remember, everyone in a company can answer, "Yes, I'm the decision-maker," even if not the final authoritative decision-maker.

Question #2 assumes you are with the final decision-maker and even if you are wrong, the chances are real good that they will not correct you.

Only Question #3 gives the prospect the room, the respect and the encouragement to answer honestly and completely. Question #3 is the best.

8. What is my best course of action? Do I have any alternatives that will give me a higher value? Once people agree that they have a need, they will naturally start considering options to have the need either fulfilled or eliminated. It's normal for them to be more open to suggestions, and it's natural for them to want the best course of action.

Sometimes, the best course of action is self-evident. Sometimes, your prospect will not know and will be open to your leading if you have earned their respect and if you have earned the right to tell him or her what to do.

Doctors are very good at telling patients what must be

done. Doctors earn the right to tell us what to do by asking questions, listening, making a diagnosis and then defending their diagnosis with product knowledge when necessary.

It is an interesting parallel to selling that a doctor's credibility is enhanced as much by the questions they ask as by the things they tell us. In fact, if doctors do not ask good questions and then listen, we probably will not listen to them later when they tell us what we must do.

The best way to earn the right to provide the best course of action is to thoroughly understand your prospect's need. You do this best by asking questions, listening and then matching their need with your products or services by using your product knowledge and even more questions.

Everyone and everything has competition. Even if it's just the momentum that causes prospects to not want to change. You do not have to overcome all competition or alternatives that your prospect may have. You only have to show that your solution has greater value than their current best solution.

You must be ready to identify (with questions) their current best solution and then, demonstrate how your solution will bring greater peace of mind. You don't buy from the best or the cheapest doctor . . . you buy from the one who gives you the greatest level of confidence that he or she knows what they are doing. It's the same in selling. You buy from the one who gives you the greatest level of confidence that he or she knows what they are doing. You must be ready to be that person.

9. What will it cost? Obviously you need to be able to answer this question, but less obviously, you need to know what other pricing options are available.

Natural Selling Concepts

Every buyer knows that good salespeople can raise or lower their price if there is a good reason. You can raise your price if your prospect's commitment or quantity decreases or if the required level of service increases. You can lower your price if your prospect's commitment or quantity significantly increases or if the required level of service decreases.

10. Why should I go forward today? What will I lose (what will it cost) if I do not go forward? What will I gain (what will it add) if I do go forward? Simply stated, if purchasing your product(s) or service(s) will bring a value to your prospect (and it must!), then every day that your prospect does not have your product(s) or service(s) is a day of lost value.

Several years ago, I made sales calls with a gentleman who sold manufacturing equipment and systems. He also sold less tangible things like service agreements, installation and training. One of our calls was to a company in Northern Ohio that needed a new piece of production equipment.

After introductions, the buyer stated that they had decided to upgrade one of their production lines, and they would like this salesman's company to be one of three bidders. He went on to say that they had researched eight or nine manufacturers and was convinced that the three chosen companies were the best of the group. He further stated that he knew our pricing would be similar to the other two bidders and in the "quarter-million-dollar" range.

The prospect said he wanted a proposal submitted within two weeks and then would make a decision within another four weeks. Then, he said, "After we award the contract, we will want installation and training to be completed within six additional weeks."

The salesman paraphrased, "So you're going out to two other possible suppliers and asking for proposals, and you want to be totally up to speed in twelve weeks?"

The prospect nodded and said, "That's correct."

The salesman asked, "Once this new equipment is in place, will it lower your cost, or will it increase your sales?" The buyer looked a bit puzzled, then slowly stated, "I guess initially it will save us money because we will virtually eliminate overtime. But eventually, it will increase sales and profitability because we will have greater capacity and will be back on overtime at the higher capacity as soon as that happens."

The salesman asked, "How much will it save initially?"

The prospect again looked a bit puzzled, then opened his top left desk drawer and removed a computer report. He leafed through several pages and pointing at something I couldn't see, said, "I guess it will initially save us about $6,000 per day in overtime."

The salesman once again paraphrased, "So you are going to take six weeks at $6,000 per day to make a decision and then spend approximately $250,000 to be up to speed in a total of twelve weeks?"

The prospect nodded slowly.

Then the salesman said, "That's $6,000 per day or $42,000 per week or $252,000 for overtime for the next six weeks plus your estimated $250,000 purchase price for a total investment of $500,000 . . . is that correct?" The prospect slowly nodded.

We walked out with the order after the salesman said, "You've done your research . . . you already know we can do the job . . . wouldn't it be better to go forward today and save the $252,000 overtime and get to the higher sales sooner?"

The salesman closed the order by converting the cost of waiting into lost value.

Natural Selling Concepts

Always be ready to show the buyer why it is more to their advantage to go forward than to wait.

Once you are ready to answer the ten questions, how do you best prepare your presentation?

You can use visuals, demonstrations, testimonials, samples, videos, etc. You can do a presentation face to face, voice to voice, via teleconference or you might fax, e-mail or overnight it. There are millions of ways to do presentations. However, by definition, there is only one *best* way!

The *best* way follows a very simple outline . . .

- Start with the decision you want the prospect to make. List all of the possible reasons they might not make a decision to give you their business.

- Decide which of the ten questions you need to answer during the presentation in order to get the prospect to make a positive decision. These will usually be spelled out in the Up-Front Contract.

- List your resources and decide how much time, effort and money you should invest in the proposal.

- Plan what you are going to say and do.

- Practice on someone who can give objective feedback.

- Be ready (a) to test the water for objections, (b) to handle objections, and (c) be ready to close . . . the next three things you need to master and the next three steps in the *Natural Selling Process.*

🌿 CHAPTER TEN 🌿
Trial Closing

When you "close" in sales, it means you are asking for the order . . . You are asking your prospect to make a commitment . . . to make a final decision. *Trial* closing is not asking for a commitment, it is only asking for an opinion . . . It is not asking for a final decision.

So why would you use a trial close instead of just going for the decision? The answer is timing, and understanding it is critical to becoming a great closer.

It's important for you to know that the timing is right before asking your prospect to make a decision. If your timing is off . . . if your prospect still has objections that you haven't addressed and is not ready to say "Yes," you could actually endanger the sale by trying to close. Trial closing is "testing the water" to make sure your prospect is ready to say, "Yes."

Remember that people are "wired" or programmed. How did you remember that Mary had a little . . ? You remembered it because you are wired. You are programmed so that whenever you hear "Mary had a little . . ." you automatically think, *lamb.*

Your prospect's decision-making wiring is just as predictable.

There are two types of wiring to consider when getting ready to close.

The first is fairly obvious. People are wired to wait. Maybe because they aren't yet sold or maybe because they want to let the salesperson down easy. They say, "I want to think it over . . . Let me get back to you . . . I want to sleep on it . . . Your prices are too high . . . I have a friend or relative in the business . . . I have to talk it over with my spouse . . . etc." People are not wired to reject other people and that's why they feel they need to have a reason to say no to a salesperson.

The second type of wiring relates to a prospect's ego and their natural desire to be correct. When a person makes a decision, they assume ownership of the decision and naturally, want to be right. Whether it's good or bad, they become less objective and more predisposed (wired) to defend their decision.

Put the two types of wiring together and you have normal prospects. They don't want to make decisions, but once they do, they don't want to change their mind.

That's why you need to trial close. You need to make sure your timing is right and your prospect is ready to say, "Yes!" If your prospect is going to say, "No," then it's not the best time to close.

NATURAL SELLING CONCEPT #19

The best time to close is when your prospect is ready to say yes.

For example, if you were to ask a prospect, "Which do you prefer, Option A, or Option B?" and the prospect responds, "I don't care for either option," you know it's not the best time to close. However, if the prospect says, "I really like Option B," you could immediately close with, "Great, let's write it up."

Trial Closing

Trial closing helps you know the answer to the timing question. If your prospect responds affirmatively, you are ready to close. If your prospect says anything but "Yes," probe to identify their remaining objections. Once you have identified whatever objection might have been hidden and causing your prospect to hesitate, go for a new Up-Front Contract to confirm you are correct. As soon as you have "Yes" to your Up-Front Contract, fill your half of the contract *(Chapter 9: Presenting)* and proceed to the close.

NOTE:

Trial closing is a great way to transition from the presentation to the close. It's also a great way to surface any remaining objections that might sidetrack you later.

An Up-Front Contract is not the same as a trial close. An Up-Front Contract asks for a commitment to move forward and may even be a close contingent on your filling your half of the contract. A trial close asks for an opinion so you can learn if your prospect is ready to move forward *before* you ask for the commitment.

Don't nudge a person who is sitting on
a fence until you have given
(and confirmed) a good reason for him
to be leaning toward <u>your</u> side.

–C. Bromer

❧ CHAPTER ELEVEN ☙

Working Through Objections

What exactly is an objection? It's any reason or excuse a prospect gives for not going forward with the sale. There is no question whether or not you will face them. You will! The only questions are: "When?" And, "Will you have a lamb ready?"

First, the bad news — objections are like the obstacles in an obstacle course. They do not speed you up. They aren't the easiest part of the obstacle course. You will encounter them, like it or not. And, if you ignore one, you'll probably regret it . . . you might even be disqualified.

NATURAL SELLING CONCEPT #20

Objections are not a good sign! It is much easier to avoid having prospects build them than it is to overcome them! Even excellent salespeople run into them. However, you will avoid most standard objections if you follow the *Natural Selling Process*.

Now, the good news — if you know all of the possible obstacles . . . and, if you have a best way to handle each one . . . and, if you practice each best way until it becomes an automatic best response, then the next time you face any of those obstacles, you will do your best in handling them.

That's your challenge in working through objections. Know all of the objections that you might face and have a lamb prepared for each one.

Natural Selling Concepts

You're probably thinking, "Get real! There are millions . . . maybe billions of possible objections! How can I possibly list all of them? And since there are millions . . . maybe billions of ways to respond to each objection, how can I possibly know the best way to handle each one?"

Before I answer that, I want you to carefully consider the following question. If I can prove to you that there really are only twenty objections that you will ever face, and that there is only one best way to respond to each objection, will you commit to internalizing those lambs so they will be automatically available the next time you need them? Will you also agree that if you have those lambs internalized, the next time you need one you will be better able to do your best?

That was an Up-Front Contract! If you said yes, you are ready to proceed. If you said no, go back and read it again; and if you still say no, then lay this book aside until you decide to make a commitment to be your best.

Now, for some great news!

There really aren't millions of objections. The actual number is very small. In fact, all objections fall into one of only eight categories. If we count subtle variations and specific objections that you might hear in your industry, you might end up with as many as thirty specific variations within the eight categories. Once you know all of the objections (obstacles) that you might face in your particular industry or job, you'll be ready to build a lamb for each.

Where do you start?

Before I give you the list of objection categories, I would like you to do an exercise. It will take less than five minutes and it will be a real eye-opener for you. I would like for you to list every objection you have ever heard. If you are new to selling, I would like you to list every objection that you might give if someone were trying to sell to you. Don't start just yet . . . continue reading until I say, "Go."

Trust me, this exercise will take less than five minutes! You are going to discover a great secret: There really are only a few objections that you'll ever hear.

Now, as you compile your list, don't be redundant! Don't list:

- "Your price is too high . . ."
- "I can't afford that . . ."
- "Gee, that's a lot of money . . ."
- "I don't have it in the budget . . ."
- "That's too much to spend . . ."
- "I can get a better price from your competitor . . . etc."

Those are all the same (price) objection. Don't be redundant! However, if you are not sure if two objections are redundant, go ahead and list them both. It will be better to have a little redundancy than to possibly miss one.

Set an alarm or timer for five minutes and go ahead with the exercise now.

Assuming you did the exercise, you now know something that most professional sales people don't even suspect. You now know that there really aren't millions and millions of objections. You now know that there really are only a finite number of objections and you probably learned it in the first two to three minutes of the exercise.

Now I'm going to let you in on another secret. If you did the exercise without peeking forward, you may not have even listed the number one objection in your industry. It's the number one objection in every industry! That number one objection is: "I want to think it over." It comes in many forms:

- "Let me get back to you . . ."
- "I'm not ready to make a decision just yet . . ."

- "I need to sleep on it . . ."
- "I want to check out a couple of other options . . ."
- "Let me talk it over with (someone else) . . . etc."

All of these objections are stall tactics. If you eliminate the redundancy, you could restate them all as the following single objection: "I'm not going to make a decision right now because I'm not ready!"

Go back and look at your list and make sure you have as little redundancy as possible and add the "stall" objection if you don't already have it.

At this point, you probably have fewer than sixteen objections listed. The actual number is not important. What is important is that you have probably listed 98% or more of all the objections you typically face and as soon as you internalize a lamb for each, you will be ready to professionally face 98% or more of all of the objections you will ever hear.

What if other objections come up that you haven't listed?

Natural Selling Concept #21

Whenever you hear a new objection, make a note of it. Then, if you hear it two times, develop a lamb.

The balance of this chapter is dedicated to showing you how to develop lambs . . . and showing you some standard lambs that have already been developed.

Before developing lambs, there are some things you need to know:

1. All decisions involve comparing perceived benefits to perceived costs. Perceived benefits are what your prospect believes he will gain: peace of mind, emotional well-being, safety, convenience, quality, efficiency, productivity, competitive advantage, profit, etc. Perceived costs are what your prospect believes he or she will have to pay: money, time, effort, risks to existing relationships, risks associated with working with you, etc.

Costs and benefits control decisions. Negative decisions are the result of perceived costs outweighing perceived benefits. Positive decisions are the result of perceived benefits outweighing perceived costs. Even snap decisions and intuitive decisions are based on the perceived differences between benefits and costs.

This relationship between costs and benefits is often referred to as "value."

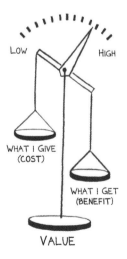

Figure 11-1: Cost — Benefit — Value

2. People never make buying decisions based on price alone. People do not buy price. They buy value.

NATURAL SELLING CONCEPT #22

$$\text{Value } \alpha \ \frac{\text{Quality } \times \text{ Service}}{\text{Price}}$$

α = "Is directly proportional to"

Perceived value is directly proportional to the quality of what you sell multiplied by the service you and your company provide and inversely proportional to total price. (Total price includes cost, convenience, time invested, etc.)

When someone says, "Price is the only issue," they're really saying, "You haven't convinced me that you're any different from your competitors." However, even if you are selling a commodity that's available everywhere, and even if you're selling it mail order with no apparent personal touch, you are still going to provide a different value. Your service will be greatly impacted by you . . . and nobody has you . . . except you!

3. Price is a major objection area in most industries for two reasons. First, price is a great way to get rid of Webster salespeople. Remember, Webster salespeople are the ones who are rude, crude and obnoxious . . . generally unprofessional and definitely not interested in the customer . . . only themselves. Webster salespeople have another characteristic that makes them vulnerable to the price objection. They are usually more interested in not losing than they are in winning. There is a difference!

People who do not want to lose (Webster salespeople)

are always looking for excuses when they fail. They don't feel they are failing if they have a good excuse to take back to the person to whom they report. They feel they are not losing if they can say,

"It's not my fault; our price is too high."

"It's not my fault; our last order was messed up in production."

"It's not my fault; it's everyone else's."

Winners are different.

They are the ones who, after losing a sale, come back and say to their manager or coworker, "I lost the order. There has to be something I can do better the next time. Let me explain what I did and what happened. Maybe you can give me some ideas on how I might do better the next time." Winners are more interested in winning than in not losing!

The second reason that price is a major objection area is that prospects like to have logical reasons for everything they do and price is a logical way to justify not going forward.

4. People have different buying motives. People have different reasons for buying. However, they all have the same "predominant buying motive." They all want peace of mind.

They want to know that they will receive good value for what they pay. Your job is to find needs that your products and services can satisfy, and fill them in such a way that you and your prospect both make a profit or gain. Sound familiar? If you have done everything properly up to this point in the *Natural Selling Process*, you will have identified the needs that fit our definition of selling.

WHAT DO PROSPECTS REALLY BUY?

PEACE OF MIND!

Moreover, you will have given your prospect the peace of mind that comes from him knowing that you understand his specific situation.

5. Never use someone else's words. We each have individual conversational style. Some people talk fast — others slowly. Some use the "King's English." Others speak "Good ole boy." You will do your best if you focus on being *your* best, not *someone else's* best.

6. The <u>best</u> safeguard against objections is having a good relationship with your prospect. If your prospects were close relatives who really loved you, would you assume they would go out of their way to help you make sales? There's no doubt. You know they would! They would go out of their way to help you to eliminate obstacles or objections. If you have competition, your relative would probably let you know everything about them so you could most appropriately adjust your approach to counter their strengths or exploit their weaknesses.

Having a great relationship with your prospect doesn't guarantee there will be no objections. It does, however, reduce the number of objections, and it helps you to work through them with a positive outcome.

7. The <u>best</u> answer to an objection is one that gets the salesperson back on "safe ground." When prospects object, they are essentially saying, "I'm not going to go on from here." They're saying, "You are no longer on safe ground because, in my mind, I am no longer buying."

An effective, best answer will do two things: (a) It will get you back on safe ground, and (b) It will get the sale moving forward again. (If moving forward is still possible.)

Working Through Objections

It's been my experience that a majority (as high as 95%) of sales can be moved forward after a first objection. A high percentage of second and third objections can also be moved forward — assuming you have appropriate professional lambs.

Now you're ready to develop lambs. Let's look at a couple of ways to build them, and then how some fairly standard lambs have already been developed.

Go back to the list of objections that you developed earlier. Start with the one that is probably your most common objection: "Let me think it over."

The three-step lamb-building approach

1. Acknowledge the objection. ("I don't blame you for being concerned.") Do not disagree or argue or imply that the prospect might be right or wrong. Some people believe it is okay to ignore a prospect's first objection. Don't do it! I have never been impressed with anyone who ignored me. If you have ever been ignored, you know what I'm talking about.

2. Shift to a "probing mode." ("Let me ask a couple of quick questions.") The purpose of Step 2 is to get you back into a need-finding mode, because obviously you haven't found enough of a need for the prospect to want to go forward. Or, you haven't identified enough value for the needs you have found. Either way, you need to get back on safe ground — back to asking questions.

3. Probe until you identify enough need and enough value, or the real competition (or alternative). Then go back for another "Up-Front Contract."

This is a powerful approach to all objections.

Natural Selling Concepts

Let's review, with possible lambs:

Let's assume we just heard, "Let me think it over," or "I'd like to sleep on it before I make my decision," or "Let me get back to you." As I mentioned earlier, there are millions of ways the objection can be verbalized, but they all boil down to the same thing: "I'm not ready to make a decision."

Step 1: Acknowledge

- "I can understand your not wanting to make a hasty decision."
- "It is an important decision and I don't blame you for wanting to be sure."
- "You're wise not to be too hasty on a decision like this."

  Remember, your objective is to acknowledge. Not to argue or disagree.

Step 2: Probe

- "What is causing you the most concern?"
- "Usually, when people hesitate to make a decision, it's a sign that they have some unanswered questions. What questions do you have that are causing you to hesitate?"
- "What questions are slowing you down?"

  Then, continue to probe until you can go to Step 3.

Step 3: Go back for another "Up-Front Contract."

Assuming your prospect said they wanted to wait until they knew they could "afford it," you would know that you just uncovered an objection that wasn't acknowledged earlier. Your new Up-Front Contract might sound something like,

- "So, you would go forward, but first you need

to see that the cost is more than justified and
you have a way to pay for it?"
Or, you might say,
- "If we could show that it actually pays for
  itself, would that help you to go forward?"

There are many different ways you can verbalize the
Three-step. Be sure to use your own words, and be sure to
practice. It's a great idea to practice with coworkers or your
spouse. The more you practice, the more comfortable you
will be. If you practice enough, you will be able to focus
more on what your prospect is saying and doing than on
how you are going to respond.

More lamb-building approaches
Another approach to building lambs is called the "feel-
felt-found" method.

Proponents of this method suggest saying something
like: "I understand how you feel. Others initially felt the
same way. But, they found that . . ." Then you are supposed
to introduce some new evidence to help the prospect to
change their mind. This approach has been around for a
long time and it might be effective in some circumstances.
It often falls short, though, because it doesn't encourage or
allow the prospect to verbalize their real objection. If the
real objection is hidden as in the previous example, the
feel-felt-found method will not help.

Another approach that I recommend is to list all of the
objections you have ever heard more than once and
develop a lamb for each. Refer back to your list. If you have
eliminated redundancy (variations of the same objection)
you know there really only are a few that you will ever hear.
There may be millions of variations, but there really are
remarkably few objections.

Natural Selling Concepts

One other fact — The objections will be essentially the same, no matter what products or services you sell.

No matter which approach you use, there will be times when you are knocked off balance or caught by surprise with an unexpected objection, one that you are not prepared to address. You go into mental vapor lock; your mouth opens but nothing comes out. If this ever happens, use the following lamb: Raise your eyebrows and say, "Oh?"

That one-word question obligates your prospect to keep talking and explain more. It gives you time to think and, hopefully, respond more appropriately. It's an excellent lamb and the first one you should commit to memory.

Now, let's look at the standard objections that you already know you are going to hear when you sell.

I have grouped them into eight basic categories and then given several variations of each along with strategies and at least one possible lamb. Remember that the exact words aren't as important as understanding the guiding principles and subsequently developing your own lambs. The first two objections may be answered with the same lambs.

Eight categories of objections:
1. No Need . . .

2. No Want . . .

(Use the same approach to both . . .)

Objection: "I don't see a need for your product (service, system, etc.)."

Strategy: Probe to understand your prospect's perception of their current need and how much they know about available solutions (including your solution).

Lamb: "If I were in your shoes, I might feel the same

way. May I ask you a few questions to see if you're okay with your current method (product, service, system, etc.) or if now might be a good time to consider a better approach?"

Objection: "We're not ready to make any commitments. We have to make some (internal) changes first."

Strategy: Give the prospect a reason to see you while they are waiting.

Lamb: "Before you make internal changes, we need to talk. It's important that you make a good decision based on up-to-date information. Let's set a time to get together so we can show you some things that will help you to make the best decision. How does (date) and (time) look for you?"

Objection: "We're not busy right now . . . Our business is down . . . We're not big enough to need your service (product, system, etc.) . . ."

Strategy: Appeal to their need for more business. Find out what your prospect's goals really are. Demonstrate how your product, service, system, etc., will save time or money and allow the individual to achieve the goals.

Lamb: "It sounds like you wouldn't mind having more business . . ?" (Wait for response) Then, probe on goals until you find the real (personal) reasons for growth. These are the reasons that will cause the prospect to take action. Profit may be the stated goal, but the real goal is more in the area of what the profit will do for the person.

Objection: "We're going to do this project in-house."

Strategy: Your prospect is saying, "We can do this ourselves." There are several possibilities: Maybe they want to save time or money . . . Maybe they want to control the quality . . . Maybe they just want to check their internal costs with someone on the "outside."

You should probe to find out why they decided to do it themselves and what their in-house capabilities are. When they give you the reason for keeping the work in-house, it will typically relate to one or more of the above issues. Once you know, immediately go for an Up-Front Contract.

Lamb: "So, you are saying, if we could (save time; save money; provide higher quality; etc.), you would still consider using us?"

Alternate Lamb: "Maybe we can support you on this; let me ask a few questions to . . ."

3. No time . . . No hurry . . . Want to wait . . .

Objection: "I have other higher priorities."

Strategy: Find out what the prospect's plans and priorities really are. Show how the value gained from working with you might bring a greater benefit than some of their current priorities. The value gained from working with you might even help them to achieve or afford their other priorities quicker."

Lamb: "It sounds like you have some important goals. May I ask what they are?" (Probe until you find out if the benefit to working with you outweighs the benefits they will receive from their current priorities.)

Objection: "We're too close to year-end (or some other event). Check back later."

Strategy: Show the prospect there's more value in going forward than in waiting — or — come back later. (That second option is for Webster salespeople early in a call or professionals who have exhausted all other options.)

Lamb: "We can do that, but first may I ask you a couple of questions to make sure it's worth your time and mine to get back together at a later date?" (Probe to find how much value the prospect might be losing by waiting.) If your product or service will bring a benefit to the prospect, and it must, then every day that the prospect goes without it brings some loss.)

Objection: "Let me think it over. I'll get back with you."

Strategy: Realize that there are only two reasons for waiting. Either your prospect still has questions or they have something that they aren't going to tell you. Sometimes prospects have secrets. Sometimes they are working closely with a relative who just happens to be your competitor. Sometimes they don't like the look on your face. Maybe you look like someone who beat him up in the second grade and, even though he no longer remembers why, he just doesn't like your "look." Sometimes, prospects don't have the authority to decide, but their ego is preventing them from admitting it. Many biases and prejudices can impact your prospect and you may have little chance of changing them.

However, based on my own experience, 95% of all stalls are actually due to questions that the prospect has that haven't been answered; questions like:

"Can I afford it?"

"Is it the best for my money?"

"Do I need it now?"

"Can it wait?"

Knowing this, we can create a lamb that addresses the 95% and even helps the prospect to open up a bit on the other 5%.

Lamb: "I don't blame you for not wanting to make a hasty decision. However, it's been my experience that when a person hesitates, it's usually because they still have unanswered questions. What questions do you have that are making you want to wait? Maybe I can answer some of them today and perhaps get a bit closer to a decision. What questions do you still have?"

Another Strategy: List all of the advantages of going forward and compare them with the cost of waiting. (You should be prepared to show prospects that it's always better to move forward than to wait!)

4. No money . . . Price way too high . . .
Before we attack the value issue, consider the following:

NATURAL SELLING CONCEPT #23

When working through price objections, remember that nobody ever buys or sells anything for what it is really worth. People buy based on their *perception* of the facts that they know, not based on *all* of the facts. If people only bought after knowing *all* of the facts, we would all be driving the same kind of car!

Objection: "Your prices are way too high!"

Strategy: Caution! When a prospect claims your price is way too high, it is a common mistake to assume that the prospect is comparing your product or service with something that must be inferior. I have heard numerous seasoned salespeople respond with, "Are you sure we're quoting apples for apples?" This is a terrible thing to ask! It essentially says, "Are you sure you know what you are talking about; are you sure you really know your job?" It's an insult! There is a much better lamb. Your strategy should be to point out that you might have made a mistake, and you need to ask more questions to make sure you did not.

Lamb: "(Prospect's name), usually when there's a price difference that large, it means someone made a mistake. Maybe it was me . . . maybe it was my competitor. Let me ask you a couple of questions to make sure I didn't make a mistake in my pricing."

(Actually, the error may have been on the part of the prospect, but there's no benefit to you in pointing out that possibility.) Then probe to find out why there's a large price difference.

Strategy Post-Script: *If your competition decides to give products or services away, you can't stop them. If your competition makes mistakes in pricing, you can't stop them. If your competition suddenly gets stupid, you can't stop them. We have laws in America against everything except stupidity. Sometimes when competitive prices are significantly lower for no significant reason, you just have to walk away.*

Always check with your management first to make sure you aren't "missing" something.

Alternate Strategy: *(Qualify) Too high compared with what? Too high compared to other products or services? Too high compared with what was budgeted?*

Compare what you're offering (features and benefits) with your competitor. Then you have three choices:
(a) Demonstrate how your product or service is superior (raise the perceived value),
(b) Lower your price, or
(c) Lose the order.
Sometimes, you may try a combination of (a) and (b) in order to avoid (c).

Lamb: "When there's a significant price difference, there's usually also a performance difference. Let's look at your other (product or service) and compare what you are actually getting with what you are paying."

Natural Selling Concepts

5. No money . . . Price a little too high . . .

Objection: "Your price is off by (x)%."

Strategy: Whenever a prospect tells you how much you differ from a competitor, you should assume the order may be yours already. Follow the four steps below to make sure you do your best.

Lamb: "Is that going to stop you from going forward?"

If your prospect responds, "No," write up the contract! A finite number of times, your prospect will respond with, "No, it will not stop us, but it would be nice if you could lower your price," or, "No, I just wanted you to know since I'm paying more to work with you I will expect better service." In other words, the order is yours, you can lower your price if you want — but you don't have to.

If your prospect responds with, "Yes," . . . ask, "How far off do you feel we are?" Then proceed with the strategy below.

Lamb: "Are you saying we have to come all the way down to that price?"

At this point, there is a 95% chance that your prospect will answer, "No, but you do have to get closer." In other words, you hardly ever have to match a competitor's price when your prospect tells you you're, "off by x %."

If your prospect answered, "Yes," you would respond with:

Lamb: "So you're saying we can have your business if we match that price?"

If your prospect answered, "No," to that question, respond with:

Lamb: "Where do you feel our pricing would need to be for you to work with us?" (CAUTION: Do not offer to lower your price. At this point, you are probing to see where the prospect's perception of your value is versus your competition. Also, you are testing to see if price is a real objection or a smoke screen. If it is a smoke screen, your prospect will introduce a new objection at this point.)

Objection: "Our business has been slow." "I'm concerned about the economy." "I don't know what the market is doing."

Strategy: Get the prospect to focus on the future, not on the past or even the present.

Lamb: "There are two great reasons to go forward in a down economy: First, it's more important than ever that you have the most efficient operation. You can't afford to be less than your best in an economy that punishes stragglers. Second, you know the economy will change. It always does! Now is the time to invest in (x) so you will be ready for the next growth cycle."

6. No trust . . . We don't know you . . .

Objection: "I have been doing it this way for years. I don't like change."

Strategy: Probe to see what goals can be reached if the prospect makes the change. Help the prospect to understand that not accomplishing goals and not achieving optimum profitability are even more uncomfortable.

Lamb: "I don't blame you! Change is uncomfortable. A good rule of thumb is to never change anything — improve it or leave it alone! Let's talk about what kind of improvement you can expect with our (product/service). If the benefit doesn't more than make up for the slight discomfort, I wouldn't blame you for not changing. By the same token, if there were a good benefit, you wouldn't want to miss it. Let me

Natural Selling Concepts

ask you a few quick questions." (Then proceed with probing questions as previously mentioned.)

Objection: "Why should I buy your product?"

Strategy: Early in the call: get permission to probe. Late in the call: summarize reasons to go forward today.

Lamb: (If it happens early in a sales call . . .) "I'm not sure you should; let me ask you some [need-finding and probing] questions . . ."

(If it happens late in a sales call) "Let's summarize the reasons to go forward today . . ." (This assumes that you would have identified some benefits by "late in the call.")

Objection: "Your competitor is closer to our location," or "You don't have an office in our area."

Strategy: Probe to point out that living close does not necessarily mean good service. Use caution: This may be the prospect's way of saying your competitor is a personal friend. If the prospect and your competitor are good close personal friends, get with your manager to decide what strategy to employ.

Lamb: "Are you concerned with response time, our level of service, convenience, shipping charges, etc?

"If we could prove to you that our (response time, level of service, convenience, shipping charges, etc.) will not negatively impact you, would you be willing to work with us?"

Objection: "I have been with your competitor for years, and they do a good job for us." (In other words, "I don't trust you as much as I trust them.")

Strategy: Sell the prospect on replacing their current solution with one better designed for their particular needs or better designed to grow as they grow — OR on having two suppliers.

Lamb: "It sounds like you have a great relationship and I don't blame you for not wanting to rock the boat. Let's look at the advantages and disadvantages of having two (or more) solutions? How does (date) and (time) look for you?

Objection: "Other people in our industry use your competitor."

Strategy: Position your company (products or services) as "above" the cloud of "wannabe's."

Lamb: "You don't want to be like the other people in your industry . . . you're better than that! (pause) It's true that some of your competitors use our competitors, but none of those products or services come close to ours when it comes to helping you grow and be more profitable. Let me ask you a few questions to see if our system would be more of what you really need . . .

Objection: "You don't have the most current products or services."

Strategy: Don't be surprised, and don't act upset. In fact let the prospect know that when you are on top with the best product, it's not unusual for competitors to say untrue things about you or your company.

Lamb: "I'm sure our competitors wish that were true. Where did you hear . . ? They may have us confused with one of our competitors."

7. No trust . . . We *do* know you . . .

Objection: "I have heard negative things about your reputation. I've heard bad things about you from your former customers. A friend of mine at (Company) uses your (product/service), and he's not happy with it. Your company doesn't deliver what you promise."

Strategy: If you ever hear such things, they are either fact or rumor. Either way, you need to deal with them with extreme urgency. Anything less communicates that they are true and that you don't care.

Non-specifics should be handled as though they were rumors started by competitors. Do not fight against unsubstantiated rumors. Just smile, and acknowledge that some competitors would like to see you fail. Some might even make up stories.

Probe for "specifics." Any negative comment that can be traced to a known source or competitor should be reported to management for strategy development or possible legal action if you or your company are being slandered or libeled.

Lamb: (If specific sources are cited) "Let me get some details so we can address this."

(If your prospect is vague and doesn't have the specific source) "I'm sure our competitors wish that were true. Let's look at the real facts . . ." Give proofs and probe to make sure your prospect is back "in the boat" with you.

Objection: "I don't like your company."

Strategy: Probe! Do not attempt to answer this or any other question until you "hear it" fully.

Lamb: "I'm sorry to hear that, but there has to be a reason that you feel this way. Would you please share it with me?"

Then probe until you can go for the following Up-Front Contract . . . "I appreciate your sharing this with me. If we can fix (whatever the problem was) to your satisfaction, would you be willing to work with us again?"

Objection: "Your accounting department messed up my billing . . . I had bad experiences with your company in the past . . . Your support has been terrible . . . The previous salesperson was a jerk . . ."

Working Through Objections

Strategy: Apologize for the difficulty and then probe to get all of the details. Do not admit that you made a mistake until you are sure that your company did. If you admit to an error too quickly, it will not be taken as sincere or it will be taken as an admission that you knew about the problem and haven't fixed it. Attempt to solve the problem, and whenever you can't, commit to get back as soon as possible. Then get with management to develop a strategy to mend fences.

Keep in mind that not all complaints are legitimate. For this reason, do not commit to fix the problem. The problem may be beyond your authority to fix. Only commit to "get back" after you have researched the problem. (Sometimes, you will run into complainers only to discover later that the prospect created the problem — or worse, they do not pay their bills and want to make you out to be the bad guy.)

Lamb: "I'm sorry you had a bad experience. That's not the way we like to do business. If there's any way we can make it right, we need to do that. Please tell me what happened so we can address it." (Ask questions to fully identify the problem(s) . . . then commit to get back.)

Objection: "You're too small."

Strategy: Change the focus from you — to the job.

This objection is often caused by a marketing message or salesperson that gives the perception that you are too small to properly handle certain jobs. The real question is, can we do this as good as anyone else?

Lamb: "Let me ask you about the criteria of the job. Then, if we could verify our credentials and prove to you that we can more than handle this job, would you be open to giving us the opportunity?"

Objection: "We need more experience (expertise) on

this project," — or — "We have no confidence in your . . ."

Strategy: Probe, then go for an Up-Front Contract.

Lamb: "Help me understand your concerns."

(Wait for answer.) Then . . .

"So what you're saying is, you would work with us, but first we need to show you . . ."

8. Legitimate Constraints . . .

Legitimate constraints (going out of business, moving, filing Chapter 11, etc.) are actually "buy signs."

NATURAL SELLING CONCEPT #24
A "buy sign" is anything a buyer or prospect says that implies they will buy if you meet certain conditions.

One company that I know sells and installs paper mills. Their average sale is $10 million plus. One objection they hear is: "We have no land near a river." Apparently paper mills must be built next to rivers. This objection is actually a "buy sign."

Whenever they hear it, they now say, "If we could find a good location for your mill, would you be able to move forward?"

Objection: "Our current contract has two more years."

Strategy: Probe to find out if they are big enough for two systems or if they have opportunities that your competitors can't handle. (Then, if all else fails, position yourself to be their best option when the current contract expires.)

Lamb: "Do you have the authority to go off contract if you find something significantly better?"

Working Through Objections

Or . . . "Are all of your requirements locked into this contract?"

Objection: "We're in Chapter 11."

Strategy: Assume this is not something a prospect would brag about, and go for an Up-Front Contract to qualify yourself and get positioned for the close.

Lamb: "I'm not exactly sure how all that works but let me ask you . . . Are you saying you will give us the order if our accounting department can work with you through your Chapter 11 situation?"

Objection: "I want to wait for another bid."

Strategy: Attempt to be the last one in. Other bidders may raise new questions or offerings or improved scopes. Attempt to schedule another time to get back together so you can answer any new questions. The last one in is the only one who can know the whole story.

Lamb: "How soon do you want to make the final decision? [Wait for response.] Let's schedule a time to get together after you have received all of your bids to make sure we have answered all of your questions before you make your final decision."

Objection: "The scope or specification is changing on the project, so I need to wait . . ."

Strategy: Be proactive. Help the client change the scope or specification to benefit their company and your company too. Probe to understand what is changing. Once you identify the new or redefined need, go for an Up-Front Contract to confirm that you still have a qualified need.

Lamb: "If I can get you a new proposal that addresses all the aspects of this new scope, can we do business?"

Objection: "The decision will be made by a group/committee/board/etc."

Natural Selling Concepts

Strategy: *Sell your prospect on taking you to the decision-making group.*

Lamb: "(Name), there's a good chance they (the group) might ask you questions I haven't covered. Rather than you risking embarrassment by trying to answer questions I haven't covered, would it be possible for me to be there with you to answer them? I don't have to be there when they make their final decision." *(This last statement makes it easier for your prospect to take you to the group.)*

Objection: "We're under-funded — everyone's high on their bid."

Strategy: *Probe to find out how much they can spend. Talk about what you can do relative to what they can afford. You then have three possibilities:*
1. *Raise the perceived value so they will pay more for what they really need.*
2. *Lower your prices.*
3. *Lose the order.*

Go back into a need-finding mode, asking questions until you can go back for another Up-Front Contract.

Lamb: "Help me understand your pricing constraints . . ."

Objection: "Your competitor gives different reports and has better reporting systems."

Strategy: *This is the same as, "Your competitor gives better service." Probe to find out what those reports and systems are. Then go back for a new Up-Front Contract.*

Lamb: "What type of reports and reporting systems do you need? [Wait for a response.] If we could provide those reports and systems, would you . . ."

Objection: "You can't meet our schedule."

Strategy: *Assume that you are going to make the sale, but first, go for an Up-Front Contract . . . then call "time out"* *to verify you can meet their schedule. If you can't meet their schedule, attempt to discover advantages you can offer that they will have to sacrifice if they do not wait.*

Lamb: "So you're ready to go forward, but only if we can assure you that we can meet your schedule? [Wait for response.] Let me check with my people to make sure we can . . ."

Objection: "My boss has to approve this."

Strategy: Same as taking it to a group, committee, board, etc.

Lamb: "(Name), there's a good chance your boss might ask you questions I haven't covered. Rather than you risking embarrassment by trying to answer questions I haven't covered, would it be possible for me to be there with you to answer them?"

Summary

The list of objections in this chapter was not meant to be a complete list of all possible objections. It does hit on many of the more common ones.

Your mission is to:

❖ take the list of objections that you created earlier,

❖ develop a strategy for each one,

❖ then *(in your own words)* build a lamb for each one ,

❖ then . . . practice.

Practice until you can say each one so smoothly and naturally that they not only sound natural . . . practice until they *are* natural.

If you do this with the objections you listed earlier, you will become one of the best salespeople in the world.

Of course, this assumes that you also know how to close! That's the subject of the next chapter.

The objections you hear are the same
ones salespeople heard fifty years ago.
There are remarkably few . . . and they
aren't inventing any new ones.

–C. Bromer

✸ CHAPTER TWELVE ✸

Closing
(Precipitating Action)

It has been said that nothing happens until somebody sells something. Well, nobody sells anything until someone closes the order. Many salespeople are wired to wait for the prospect to close the order, but remember, prospects are wired to wait. So, that leaves it to you to close the order.

Next to dealing with objections, closing is probably the most feared part of the sales process. It's the point in the process where a salesperson can lose. Losing is interpreted as rejection and nobody likes the embarrassment of rejection.

However, it's also the point in the process where a salesperson can win and those who know how to do it best will win more than those who do not!

You need to know five things about closing:

First, you need to know what closing is.

Closing is many things. Closing is not just getting the order, though that certainly is the objective. Closing is asking your prospect to take some action — to make a commitment — to move the process forward — to make a buying decision. Closing is getting your prospect to take steps toward that ultimate goal that will be mutually beneficial for him . . . and for you.

WHY SHOULD I CLOSE?

(ANY QUESTIONS?)

Natural Selling Concepts

Closing is the focal point of the sales process. It's the point where you and your prospect agree to trade value for value. Prospecting, making the first call, establishing rapport, building a relationship, identifying needs, qualifying those needs with an Up-Front Contract, filling your half of the contract, trial closing and being ready with lambs for objections are all important because they help you to navigate to this point.

Second, you need to understand that the close will not just happen on its own . . . You need to precipitate the close . . . You need to take action!

You will miss 100% of the shots that you don't take!
–Wayne Gretzky

Several men went to a boxing match and one noticed a fighter down on one knee appearing to be praying before the first round. He asked his Christian friend what that meant. His friend looked at him, raised his eyebrows and said, "Actually, it doesn't mean anything if he can't box." Well, that's where we are in the selling process. Everything up to this point is potentially a waste if you can't (or don't) close.

Some people think you can succeed on the strength of relationships only. It's true that having a good relationship is important, but ask yourself who will be most successful: The salesperson who makes a good case for purchasing a product or service and then follows with, "Let me know if you decide to go forward;" or the salesperson with a good relationship who makes a good case for you purchasing a product or service and then follows with, "Let's get started right away . . . How does Monday look for you?"

If you want to be your best, you must develop the

ability to help people make difficult decisions. You must develop your ability to close.

Third, you need to know when to close.

The best time to close is as soon as possible. Some good times to close are right after you have:

(a)   identified a need where you and your prospect can both make a profit or a gain,

(b)   filled your half of a good Up-Front Contract that you secured earlier, and

(c)   tested the water with a trial close and found that the prospect is leaning toward the purchase.

Suppose you are meeting with a prospect in a large company and you are trying to sell him on using your service. During the call, you find that additional decision-makers will need to approve the contract. Your "new sell" is to get your current prospect to bring those other decision-makers into the process . . . perhaps even into the current meeting. If they are not available, you might prepare for your "new close" by using the following Up-Front Contract: "Let's go ahead with the balance of the presentation today. Then, if you agree that our service meets your requirements, you and I can schedule a time to get back together with the other people who will need to sign off on it. Does that sound okay?"

There are intermediate closes and a final close. Intermediate closes are decisions you ask the prospect to make on the way to the final close. When your prospect agrees to set up a meeting with the buying committee, you are making an intermediate close. When the committee agrees to accept your proposal, you are making a final close.

The complexity and pricing of your products and services will determine what a realistic sales-cycle (time from beginning to final close) might be. The longer the sales-cycle, typically the more intermediate closes you will need to do.

Fourth, you need to know the best way to close.

People who make buying decisions are often in a hurry and usually interested in saving time and money. They have little time or patience for salespeople who come in and just want to visit. They like salespeople who are brief, bright and gone! They like salespeople who understand their real needs and who know how to professionally close. They like salespeople who are professionally aggressive!

Professionally aggressive means you push for the order, but *you must first earn the right to push* by knowing as much about your prospect's business as your prospect. If you know their business and their needs really well, you will exhibit more confidence and you will be able to start sentences powerfully with, "You know what you really need to do is . . ." Your prospects will love it — if you have "earned the right."

Don't confuse building good relationships with closing. They are very different things. A good relationship helps you to earn the right to close. An excellent relationship even helps you to earn the right to professionally push.

NATURAL SELLING CONCEPT #25

You earn the right to professionally push your prospect by knowing his real needs so well that your "pushy behavior" is considered appropriate and will be *accurately interpreted* by your prospect as "genuine concern."

Closing

If you have not earned the right to push for the close, this is where everything stops. If you have followed all of the *Natural Selling Concepts* up to this point, you will have earned the right to close . . . but how do you do it?

There are a number of different ways to close.

It's important to have several ways to ask for the order. If your first attempt fails, you should probe to surface any additional concerns — then work through the concerns — and then attempt to close again. If you use the same closing question twice, it will not sound or feel right. It probably goes back to when you were younger and you heard your mother or father ask the same question two times. The second time probably made you uncomfortable because it meant they were either getting upset or they didn't believe your first answer. For whatever reason, you will not be comfortable using the same words to ask the same closing question two times in one selling situation. You need to have three or four different ways to ask for the order.

One word of caution. Every year, a new sales expert will rise to the surface with a new way to close. It has been very popular through the years for these so-called experts to claim that the "old way of selling doesn't work anymore." They say, "New prospects and old buyers are now smarter than ever and the old way of selling (we call it 'Webster selling') just doesn't work anymore." I have a news flash for these "experts." Those "old ways" never did work! Bad technique has never worked. It's true that some people buy single-sourced products from obnoxious salespeople because they have no choice, but only until it is available from another source and can be bought from someone who uses good, honest and ethical methods.

Don't confuse bad salespeople with bad closing techniques. The truth is that there are only a few best ways to ask for an order.

Natural Selling Concepts

The Nine Best Ways to Close an Order

Pick three or four of the following closing techniques. Pick the ones that are the most "natural" feeling to you. Put them into your own words and practice out loud until they become natural. Then, you're ready to close.

Each of the examples given below can be modified to be a trial close if you are not sure the prospect is ready to go forward. Remember that it's important to use your own words.

1. *Direct* — Just ask for it!
   - "May I have the order?
   - "Could you please initial our quote/proposal? "
   - "Do I have your approval to proceed?"
   - "Can we shake hands on it?"
   - "Can we get a P.O. number?"
   - "Can I get a verbal purchase order number today?"
   - "May I have your authorization to begin?"

2. *Alternate Choice* — Ask your prospect to pick one of two or three alternatives — Any choice indicates that your prospect has bought.
   - "Do you want to go with option A or with option B?
   - "Do you want to use a purchase order or just sign our agreement?"
   - "Should we start work next week or immediately?"
   - "Do we need to wait for your purchase order or can you authorize us verbally?"

3. *Minor Point* — Ask for a small decision that indicates the larger decision has already been made.
    - "Can we schedule installation for the first of next month?"
    - "Will you be our main contact once we start?"
    - "When can we start?"
    - "Can we start work immediately?"
    - "Can we get started (have approval to start) on a limited basis?"
    - "Since you're schedule-pressed, can we have an LOI (letter of intent) to start?"
    - "What if we stay over and kick off the job tomorrow?"
    - "Can we schedule a kick-off meeting for tomorrow?"
    - "When would you like us to begin work?"
    - "Can we proceed with the purchasing of equipment?"
    - "Can we go ahead and organize our resources to commence this project?"
    - "Can we get going on the engineering today?"
    - "Can I have my secretary fax a contract to sign?"
    - "Should we draw up a contract for your review?"

4. *Impending Event* — Right before asking for the order, call the prospect's attention to the fact that something bad might happen if the decision is delayed.
    - "We're near capacity; can I reserve a spot for you?"
    - "The cost will be going up soon; let's do it now!"

- "To avoid missing deadlines, can we go ahead and just bill for actual work done until the board meeting?"
- "Can I schedule the team (takes time for travel plans) to attend the kickoff meeting?"
- "Can we go ahead and schedule/reserve the team we will need to get the job done?"

Note: Some Webster salespeople use lies to create false consequences and use the "alternate choice" to manipulate prospects. If you do this, you hurt people and you become part of the problem. It's only a matter of time before you discover that you have also hurt yourself.

5. *Assumptive* — Just assume your prospect has said, "Yes," and go forward . . .
   - "We're in agreement so let's go ahead . . . Just okay the quote."
   - "Let me get some accounting information so we can set up an account for you."
   - "When will the kick-off meeting be held?"
   - "Is there anything in addition to this project that you would like us to take care of for you?"
   - "When can we expect the information so we can proceed?"
   - "What else do you need from me to process the purchase order?"
   - "When can I expect to receive the purchase order?"
   - "Let's discuss how we'll carry out the project. Let's have dinner to discuss kick-off details."
   - "I assume we have an understanding to proceed . . ? May we consider this meeting our commitment to proceed?"

6. *Step-Down Close* — This close is used after an order is all but lost. When you sense that you are going to lose and you are out of ideas, go for part of the order instead of losing it all.
   • "I accept your decision and I appreciate your having considered our company. How about allowing us to do (some smaller portion of the job)?"
   Assume that the prospect still has the option to give you a portion of the job even though they are saying you lost the job. To make the "step down" close work, you must be very close in timing to when the decision was or is being made.

7. *Summary Close* — Summarize everything that has gone before with an assumed close. This is a combination of assumptions followed by a soft, but direct close.
   • "I believe I have your scope and cost correct. My staff is ready. Will you authorize?"

8. *Old Faithful* — This is an extremely powerful close because:
   ❖ buyers can't say, no,
   ❖ it's not offensive,
   ❖ it's easy to ask,
   ❖ it's not pushy,
   ❖ it's very flexible,
   ❖ buyers like it,
   ❖ salespeople like it, and
   ❖ it's guaranteed to work.
   So, what is this magic bullet? What closing technique does all of these things? It's called "Old

Faithful" because it always works! It always gets the order or gets you closer to the order — if an order is possible. Old Faithful is a combination of a final close and a trial close. It combines an alternate choice (final close) and a minor point (trial close). There are a number of ways it can be stated:

- "Have you got yourself sold? or, do you still have questions?"
- "If you have no additional questions, let's go ahead and write it up." (Assumptive final close.)
- "Before we write this up, do you have any additional questions?"
- "Is there anything else that we should do before starting?"

Again, there are many ways you can phrase "Old Faithful." Put it into your own words. Practice it! Watch your sales go up!

9. *Hat-in-Hand* — This close is a *last resort* close. It's actually a trial close, and it is best used when all others have failed. It's especially good for reopening lost orders if the competition was fairly close and the timing is recent.

   The name comes from a time when men still wore hats. When a salesperson took their "hat in hand," it meant they were leaving. Some people might call this the "Colombo close" or the "just one more question" close. It is designed to get the prospect to tell you more than they have told you thus far. Eighty to ninety percent of the times you use this technique, the prospect will just reiterate what he has already said. But you have little to lose and in the other 10% to 20% of the cases, your prospect will tell you something new. It might sound something like this:

- "I accept your decision. However, it's been my experience that when I lose an order like this, it's usually due to one of two reasons . . . either my offer wasn't good, or I did something wrong. You said my offer was in the right area, so what am I doing wrong?"

Your prospect will almost always respond,

- "Oh, it's not you, it's just . . . " and then, ten to twenty percent of the time, they will tell you something you didn't know.

One time, at Bendix Automation, I asked my prospect the following question: "I have been calling on you for a number of months and you have stated that you liked my products and that you felt my pricing was competitive. And yet you have never bought from me. Help me understand what I'm doing wrong."

The prospect said, "Carl, it's not you. It's just . . . well did you know that Joe and Tom are first cousins?" (Joe was my competitor and Tom was the prospect's boss.) I didn't have a good lamb that would stop Joe and Tom from being cousins, so I started focusing on products and services at Bendix that Joe couldn't provide.

The "hat-in-hand" close doesn't work all the time. Nothing works all the time. It is, however, a good technique to surface hidden objections when you have tried everything else.

Fifth, you need to know the action steps to take to be your best at closing.

Your ability to close will be determined in large part by how well you have accomplished the steps in the *Natural Selling Process* up to this point. Assuming you have done everything properly, closing is the next logical step.

Closing is not a mysterious or magical skill that only the gifted possess. Like any other skill, it can be learned. Follow the outline below and you need never worry about closing again.

    a.   Pick three or four closes from the examples given earlier.

    b.   Rewrite them using your own words.

    c.   Practice them out loud looking into a mirror until you can say them naturally . . . without effort or thought.

    d.   Practice them out loud with someone you know . . . perhaps a relative or coworker. Practice until you can say them naturally, without effort or thought. Do not skip this step! Closing with a real person is significantly different from closing with a mirror.

    e.   Plan to close something in every sales call. Even if a final decision will not be possible, plan to precipitate some action that will move you closer to a final decision.

Do these things and start closing more sales!

❧ CHAPTER THIRTEEN ❧
Controlling Your Success

Y ou may not agree at first with what I am about to say, but please give it careful consideration.

You cannot control your results.
Your prospect controls your results.
The better you impact your prospect, the better your results.
What you do with your results determines your success.

The purpose of this chapter is to show you the two ways to impact prospects so you can optimize your results . . . and your success. The two ways you impact your prospects are your activity and your quality.

NATURAL SELLING CONCEPT #26

$$A \times Q \Rightarrow R$$

Activity multiplied by Quality <u>yields</u> Results

A x Q does not <u>equal</u> Results . . . it <u>yields</u> Results

Activity is what you do. It's a combination of the number of sales calls you make, the number of hours you work, the number of letters you send, the number of new prospects you see, etc. *You control your activity.*

Quality is how well you do the activity. Quality is a combination of how well you research, plan, contact, open, execute, deal with obstacles, close, follow-up, etc. *You control the quality of your activity.*

Results are subsequently *influenced* by the amount of activity multiplied by the quality of that activity.

Your <u>Activity</u> and your <u>Quality</u> influence the <u>Prospect</u>, who controls the <u>Results</u>. You do not control the results! You only influence the prospect through your activity and your quality.

If you are not achieving the results you want, your only options are to adjust your activity or your quality . . . or both.

Other things that you do not control may impact your prospect and therefore, influence your results. Things like the economy, inflation, competition, the prospect's current health, etc. You should have identified most of these things (Chapters 5, 6 and 7), and then worked through them (Chapters 8, 9, 10 and 11) prior to closing (Chapter 12).

Starting today, if you understand and appropriately apply $A \ x \ Q \Rightarrow R$ to any area of your life or career, you will do and be your best. You may not be *the* best, but you will be *your* best. That's part of the principle, too — you do not control your results, but you do control your success.

Success is being your best.

If this sounds a bit confusing, read it again and if necessary, go back to the beginning of this chapter and read it all one more time. It will be worth your effort.

$A \ x \ Q \Rightarrow R$ (Figure 13-1) is a principle that has been around since the world was created. Successful people have applied it and achieved their best. Failures have violated it, and that's why they're considered failures! To the best of my knowledge, I have never seen it written nor explained and yet, once you understand it, you will see it everywhere and you will be able to look back through history (yours and the world's) and see how it was always there.

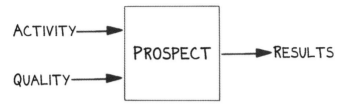

YOU CONTROL YOUR ACTIVITY (WHAT YOU DO) AND
YOU CONTROL YOUR QUALITY (HOW WELL YOU DO YOUR
ACTIVITY) YOUR PROSPECT CONTROLS YOUR RESULTS

$$A \times Q \Rightarrow R$$

Figure 13-1

When Napoleon Hill wrote *Laws of Success* in 1928, he failed to mention $A \times Q \Rightarrow R$. However, *Natural Selling Concept #26* should have been Law #17. He missed this law and one other key to success that will be covered in the last chapter of this book.

Like other laws (gravity, inertia, action-reaction, opposites attract, etc.), $A \times Q \Rightarrow R$ will be easy to take for granted. Also, like other laws, if you violate $A \times Q \Rightarrow R$, you will generate a consequence.

So the challenge is to manage your activity and your quality to get the desired best results. But here's where you run into a difficulty.

NATURAL SELLING CONCEPT #27

If you want to manage something, you have to measure it.

Activity is measurable but has an upper limit. No matter how good you are, you only get 168 hours in a seven-day week and you can only fit so much activity into that time. Quality appears to have no upper limit, but since it's based on opinion, it's difficult to accurately measure.

Since activity is limited, your *first goal must be to optimize* your activity in the time you have available. The optimum activity elements (face-to-face calls, voice-to-voice calls, letters, etc.), will be different from one industry to another. However, it's my opinion that maximizing face-to-face time with prospects during a fifty-five-hour workweek would be close to optimum. Don't get hung up on the "forty-hour workweek." It's a government creation, not a physical or mental requirement.

Since quality appears to have no upper limit, your *second goal* must be to *constantly improve* your quality. But how do you measure quality?

Most salespeople and sales managers manage quality using faulty logic. They look at results along with the activity that appeared to generate the results, and then back into assumptions about quality.

❖ Good results, good activity — Quality must be good.

❖ Good results, poor activity — Quality must be very good and it's a shame they don't work harder.

❖ Poor results, good activity — Quality must be bad.

❖ Poor results, poor activity — Quality is bad.

This is not a good way to manage yourself, or anyone else for that matter. It's management by assumption, and since it's based so heavily on results that someone else controls, it is flawed.

You can measure results, usually to the nearest penny.

You can measure activity, though few people or companies actually do. It seems many people have bought into the "work smarter, not harder" myth and now don't work hard or smart. If you want to be your best, you have to work smarter *and* harder.

You can accurately measure results and activity, but how do you accurately measure quality?

It's a problem because rating the quality of your own or someone else's behavior is subjective, subject to opinion. For example, you just made a sales call and on a scale of one to ten, you think your introduction was a nine. Your manager thinks it was a three. Which of you is right? The truth is, you're both totally correct. From your perspective, your introduction was good. From your manager's perspective, it wasn't so hot. You're both correct because you have different perspectives.

NATURAL SELLING CONCEPT #28

Without third-party feedback (someone who can share a different perspective), you cannot become your best . . . because by definition, your own blind-spots will be impossible to see.

The best way to measure quality is to:
- First, break your typical sales call down into its component parts. You may have ten parts or fifty. The number is not important. Later in this chapter, I will show you an example.
- Second, have a manager, coworker or knowledge-able friend travel with you and look over your shoulder as you make your sales call(s). It's impor-tant that they observe and not participate or interfere with the conduct of the call.
- Third, after the sales call or perhaps after a day of

sales calls, rate each of the component parts on a scale of one to ten and have your manager or friend do the same, but don't look at each other's ratings yet.

- Fourth, average your (subjective) ratings together and the final average will be more "objective" than the individual ratings. In other words, if you rate yourself on a one-to-ten scale in forty different areas and then average the forty individual parts, the average will be much more objective than the individual parts.

- Fifth, compare your overall rating and the individual parts with your manager or friend and especially note the areas where you have different ratings. The bigger the difference in an individual rating, the greater the possibility of a blind spot.

- Sixth, have someone else go with you on another sales call to validate each potential blind spot. Do this to make sure your manager or friend rated you accurately.

- Seventh, set goals, seek help and make a commitment to develop yourself in the areas where you were weakest and reevaluate yourself in four to six weeks to make sure that you have improved. In other words, repeat this seven-step process every four to six weeks.

A word of caution: Many managers cannot sit by and watch a sales call without jumping in and taking over. When that happens, it's impossible for them to give good objective feedback. If this happens, seek out a friend or coworker who can give good feedback without interfering with the call.

Two things are critical when measuring quality:

First, it is not important if the manager is right or wrong. The important thing is that if the manager saw something that generated a "low" rating, maybe the buyer saw the same thing! You cannot argue with that. The buyer's perspective may be the same as the manager's perspective.

Second, it is critical that you do not compare your rating with anyone else's. This system works best when you are comparing what your performance is . . . with what it should be, given your current experience level. The measurement is self-adjusting as you grow because it compares your quality with what it should be . . . not with some other person's quality or some arbitrary standard.

Earlier, I said the first step is to break your typical sales call down into its component parts. Again, you may have ten parts or fifty . . . the number is not important. The following example *(Figure 13-2)* lists twenty-five possibilities.

Customize the list for your business. Add components that will help measure the quality in your business. Delete those that do not apply. It's important that you include enough components to get an accurate measure of the quality of your sales call(s).

Then, use it! All management systems must eventually degenerate into work. This quality management system will work if you use it. It will not work — guaranteed — if it is not used! Remember *Natural Selling Concept #27* earlier in this chapter — "If you want to manage it, you have to measure it."

When you use this tool, always compare the quality actually observed with the quality that *should* have been observed. In other words, consider the person's experience. You might rate a new salesperson nine on question quality

Quality Measurement ⇨ Management
(Stinky) 0...1...2-Poor...3...4...5-OK...6...7...8-Good...9...10 (Superior)

Sales Quality Analysis for: _____ Date: _____

☐Self ☐Observer: _____	Rating 1-10	Comments
1	Pre-call prep. – prospect researched		
2	On time with a **Written Plan**		
3	Establishes rapport smoothly		
4	Good introductions		
5	Enthusiasm & projected confidence		
6	Grammar		
7	Smile		
8	Eye contact		
9	Brief (Focused & stayed on task)		
10	Question quality		
11	Listened to prospect		
12	Sincerity & concern for prospect		
13	Product & prospect knowledge		
14	Use of visuals (literature)		
15	Identified several needs		
16	Effective use of Up-Front-Contracts		
17	Innovative & creative		
18	Honesty		
19	Handles objections with "Lambs"		
20	**Asked for the order**		
21	Asked for the order **AGAIN**		
22	Closed the order		
23	Committed to a follow-up plan		
24	Minimum: One new name / referral		
25	Calendar/Files/Notes – Up-to-date		
	Total		

Figure 13-2: Quality Measurement Tool

Customize the list for your business or industry.

and then rate an experienced veteran five on the same questions. Why? Because you should expect more from a veteran! You should expect people to grow and to improve.

A word of caution! Do not use this quality measurement system to compare one salesperson with another salesperson. The rating is a comparison with what was observed compared with what should have been observed, given the salesperson's level of training and experience.

The value of the quality measurement system is not limited to occasional sales calls. *Natural Selling Concept #5* said, "It's not what you know that counts! It's what your habits remind you to say and do." Use the quality measurement system on a regular basis and you will not only measure quality, giving you the ability to manage it. You will also be more naturally reminded what is important by your newly developing mental habit pattern. Your habits will start reminding you about the twenty-five (or more) components that make up a best sales call. You will remember better what to say and do. You will make great progress toward being your best.

Now that you know how to manage your quality, let's look at how to manage your activity so you can optimize your results. Most people call activity-management by its more popular name, "time management."

Now that we've looked at how to measure your quality, let's look at how to measure your activity, the other thing that you control — on your way to becoming your best.

You do not control your results! Your
prospects control your results. You only
impact and influence your results with
the quality and quantity of your activity.
Work harder _and_ smarter!

–C. Bromer

❧ CHAPTER FOURTEEN ❧
Managing Your Time

Time management is really a misnomer. You are allocated an exact amount of time each day. No matter how good you are, you can't get more, and no matter how bad you are, you don't get less. No matter what anyone says, you can't save it. You can measure it, but you can't manage it.

Time management is a problem everyone talks about but nobody fixes because it doesn't really exist.

You can't manage time because you can't control it.

In the last chapter, you saw that you only control your activity and the quality that you put into your activity.

You can't manage time, but you can and you must manage the activities that you put into your time.

So how do you get your arms around the challenge to better manage the activities you put into your time? The answer lies in the definition. Most people define time management as getting more done in less time. *Natural Selling Concepts* defines it differently. We define it using four puzzle pieces that are each necessary to have a complete picture.

The first piece of the "Time Management Puzzle" is titled "GOAL."

Without a goal, time management is irrelevant. If you have no goals, you're not going anywhere, so what difference does it make how long it takes to get there?

Goals are the starting points that create the need for time management.

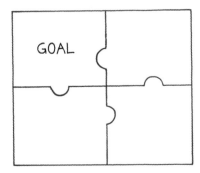

Time Management: Part 1

You probably believe that you already have goals, and maybe you do.

There are two kinds of goals: personal goals and business (vocational) goals. You must have both! However, the only reason you work is to accomplish personal goals. You will work on business goals, but only if they help you to accomplish personal goals.

If you are like most people, you have business goals that have been given to you by someone else. There's nothing wrong with these goals (sometimes called "quota"), but they will not motivate you unless they somehow tie into your personal goals.

Have you ever noticed how owners and managers seem to work harder? They're working on business goals that tie into financial goals that tie into their personal goals.

Personal goals are the key. However, most people only have very short-term and often-unspecific thoughts or dreams about what they want to accomplish. You must be different if you are going to do your *best!* Sure, you want good health, wealth, friends, success and happiness, but have you clearly defined the specifics?

Managing Your Time

Have you ever really defined the accomplishments or the activities you want to do or the amount of money you want to earn? Have you ever really defined your lifetime specific goals? If you are like most people, you expect them to eventually just happen. They might, but more often than not, they don't. Even if they do, you will probably not accomplish as much as you are capable of accomplishing, and certainly not as soon as you'd like.

The key is to define specifically what you want. So specifically and so clearly that you can see it in your mind's eye.

If you can mentally see an accomplishment or desired end, you are halfway there.

Goals that you can mentally see will pull you forward. If they're strong enough, they can even take you captive. If you graduated from high school or college, you probably experienced it, but weren't aware of it. It happened when subconsciously you changed your thinking from "if" I get my degree, to "after" I get my degree. At that point, the goal had become mentally real and visible. It was no longer an option. It would have been harder for you to stop than to go on. The goal had taken you captive.

Goals are powerful! They are keys to your motivation, your attitude and having fun. How much more do you get done when you are motivated compared to when you are not? How much more do you get done when you have a good attitude compared to when you have a bad attitude? How much more do you get done when you're having fun compared to when the job is a drudge?

You know that when you're motivated, have a positive attitude and are having fun . . . you don't just get a little more done . . . you get ten times as much done . . . maybe more!

These three things (motivation, attitude and having fun) are created by goals, and they are critical to getting the most out of your time.

Now, let's look specifically at the source of motivation.

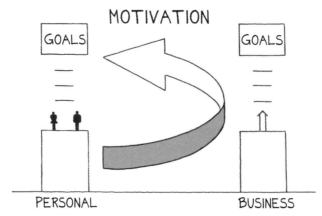

Figure 14-1: Goals are the Key to Motivation

Figure 14-1 shows two vertical bar graphs. The one on the left represents your personal history. It might be likened to your résumé. The one on the right represents the company you work for or your chosen vocation.

To the extent that you can see accomplishing your personal goals by helping your business achieve its goals — to that extent, will you be motivated to work to accomplish your business or vocational goals!

If you do not have clearly defined personal goals that excite you, it is impossible to be motivated continuously on the job. You will have ups and downs controlled by short-range goals like shelter, transportation, entertainment, food, clothing, bills, etc.

Many corporate executives believe all people should automatically have a high level of motivation just like themselves. They do not understand that business goals do not motivate!

Personal goals motivate!

Significant personal goals motivate significantly.

The excellent executive knows that motivating employees is mostly a function of helping to make sure employees have significant personal goals, understanding those personal goals and then showing them how to accomplish them by helping the business to accomplish its goals.

Goals are the key to motivation.

They're also the key to attitude. *(See Figure 14-2.)*

You will feel a positive attitude when your behavior or actions lean toward your goals. When that happens, you will naturally work harder. You will feel a negative attitude when your behavior or actions lean away from your goals.

Goals are the key to attitude. If you have no business goals, you have no *direction* to lean. If you have no personal goals, you have to *reason* to lean. You need both!

Goals are also the key to fun. Without goals, it is impossible to have real, continuous fun on the job. Think

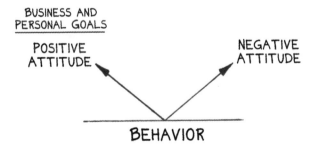

Figure 14-2: Goals are the Key to Attitude

about doing something that's fun and then ask yourself if what you're doing is accomplishing a fairly specific goal. You will be participating in something that has a clear objective . . . you will be accomplishing a goal.

Games help us to understand fun. Football, or any sport for that matter, has eight fundamentals. Take any one of the eight away and the game will vaporize instantly. These elements must also be present if you want your goals to have the power to increase your motivation, attitude and fun. Each element that you skip will be like a porthole opened in a submarine. Submarines don't have portholes, but if they did, opening one would create a negative morale factor to say the least. The sub might not sink, but it will not be its best. Leave enough portholes open, and you're going down!

The first fundamental of a well-defined, well-written goal is a clear beginning. In football, it's the kick off. In business, it's usually January 1st or the first day of the month.

The second fundamental is a clear and specific end. Normally, shorter is better. No reasonable person would sit through a football game that lasted a whole year. Yet, most company goal programs run that long. It's no wonder they lose their motivational pull sometime during the first quarter. Business goals should be guided and driven by long-range strategic objectives, but the shorter the specific tactical goals, the better.

Yearly goals drive monthly goals, which drive weekly and daily goals. Daily activity goals and individual sales call goals are best.

The third fundamental is score . . . instantaneous feedback. It's important to know exactly where you are in order to maintain the excitement necessary to have fun. If you can't measure it, you can't manage it. If you don't know where you are in relation to the finish line, you'll also lose motivation.

The fourth fundamental in goal setting is obstacles. Not having obstacles might seem positive and you could achieve results, but the achievement would be more like drudgery, not fun. Believe it or not, obstacles add the possibility of having fun.

The fifth fundamental is having a reasonable chance to win. Goals must be set reasonably because if you feel you have no chance to win, you will rationalize the goal away as "not really important anyway" or you will rationalize a new or different game.

The sixth fundamental is rules and ethics. You can win temporarily by violating rules and ethics, but it will not be permanent. And, it will not bring the joy that accompanies legitimate fun.

The seventh fundamental in goal setting is some kind of reward. Whether it's money or a promotion or only the satisfaction of knowing that you did it, you must perceive some form of reward or you will not take the action(s) necessary to accomplish the goal.

The eighth and final fundamental is a clearly defined finish point. If you have ever participated in a foot race, you know that you work harder when you are close enough to see the finish line. When you clearly see the finish line, your motivation goes up, your attitude stays up and fun can happen . . . *if* you do the other three pieces of the time management puzzle.

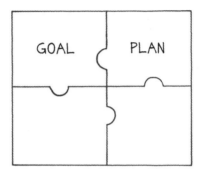

The second piece of the time management puzzle is titled "PLAN."

Time Management — Part 2

Planning in sales is critical. It's the key to productivity and the key to effectiveness.

You should plan your year, which will drive your monthly plan, which will drive your weekly and daily plans. Then comes the most critical point of all: you must plan each call. If a sales call is not worth a sheet of 8½ x 11 paper, the call isn't worth making.

When you take three to five minutes to plan a sales call, always do it in writing. It's not what you know to say and do in a call that counts, it's what you *remember* to say and do. If you have it in writing, you are much better prepared in case you go into mental vapor lock during the call.

You will not only be better prepared; you will condition the people you call on to expect you to be better prepared than most of your competitors. This fact alone makes it worthwhile! It helps to eliminate the stalls and avoidance strategies clients might use when you call for future appointments.

Planning each call *(Figure 14-3)* is the single most productive activity you can undertake in sales.

```
 1 PLAN YOUR YEAR
  2 PLAN YOUR MONTH
   3 PLAN YOUR WEEK
    4 PLAN YOUR DAY
           ↓

   5 PLAN YOUR CALL
```

DATE :_____ ACCOUNT :_____
CONTACT : _____

GOAL #1 _____
GOAL #2_____
GOAL #3_____
MATERIAL/SUPPORT REQUIRED :

NOTES:
_____ _____
_____ _____
_____ _____

↰⌐ ✗ = FOLLOW-UP REQUIRED

Figure 14-3: Planning

If you have ever been whitewater rafting, you know that the time to decide how you are going to paddle the boat is before you get vertical in the whitewater! In sales, the time to decide what you are going to accomplish in a sales call is before you make the call.

There is nothing worse than going into mental "vapor lock" in front of an important prospect. Mental vapor lock is when your brain stops functioning before you're finished with your call. You find yourself saying something clever like, "I know there was something else I wanted to cover, but I can't think of it right now." Prospects are not usually impressed with this kind of statement . . . so don't ever say it! Always have a written plan. Written is best.

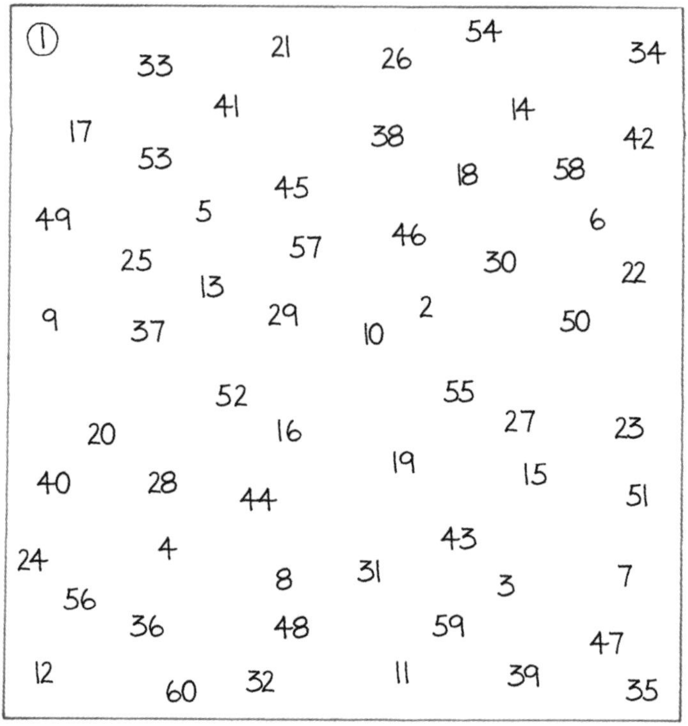

Figure 14-4: Circle Randomly Placed Numbers

Figure 14-4 shows the importance of planning. It is a box with the numbers one to sixty randomly placed throughout.

Using a watch that shows seconds, time yourself and see how quickly you can circle all sixty numbers in order. In other words, circle the number one (already circled for you in the top left corner). Then, find and circle number two, then find and circle number three, and so on until you have circled every number. Don't skip any numbers . . . they are all there! You're not competing with anyone. Just do your best and keep accurate time. Begin when you are ready.

Make a note of how many minutes and seconds it took; then go on to the next box *(Figure 14-5, next page)*. Don't look at the box until you read all of the following comments. This new box has the same numbers (one to sixty) spaced exactly like Figure 14-4, but this time they are placed in a distinct pattern. The number one is still circled and still in the upper left corner, but the number two is now somewhere in the upper right square, the number three is in the bottom right square, the number four is in the bottom left square . . . Do you recognize a pattern? Right! It's a clockwise pattern that repeats itself all the way to sixty.

Now, timing yourself again, see how long it takes to go from one to sixty. Begin when you are ready . . .

How long did it take this time? You probably circled all of the numbers in about half the time.

Why?

It's the same series of numbers, but the difference was a plan.

You had a subtle plan during the second exercise and it significantly improved your productivity

Planning is deciding ahead of time which square you will search or what you will do in a particular situation. Without planning, you will almost certainly take more time to accomplish whatever goal you have set.

The numbers illustration showed you three things. First, even a small plan increased productivity significantly. Second, obstacles created energy, not discouragement! Did you notice that when you had difficulty finding a specific number, you didn't become depressed or lethargic? You became energized and excited. The obstacles created energy because you were following a plan for a well-defined goal.

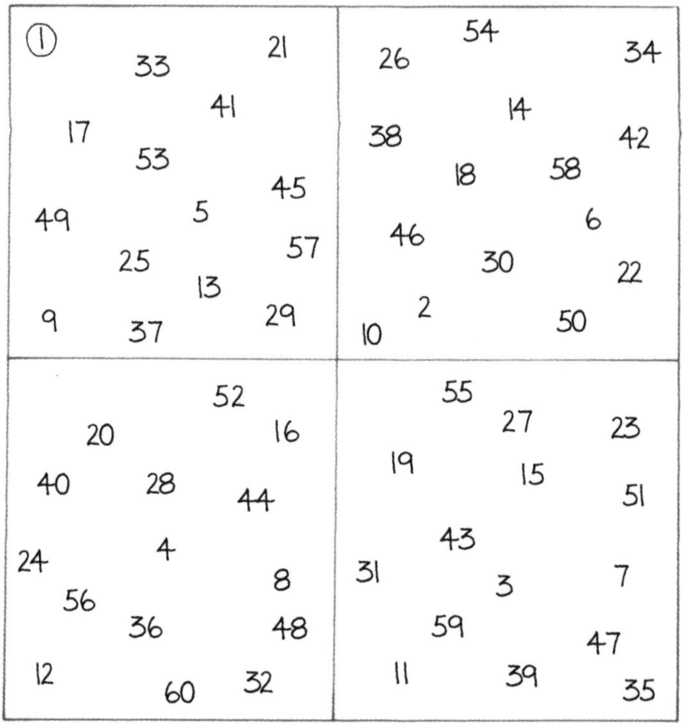

Figure 14-5: Circle Numbers Placed in a Pattern

The third thing the illustration showed was that it's fun to compete with yourself. Even though there was no reward for improvement, you naturally did your best because you understood the goal and you had a plan.

Planning is the second logical step once you set a goal.

Time Management — Part 3

Organizing is the key to efficiency. If you are not using a computer to organize your goals, plans, calendar and

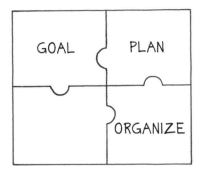

The third piece of the time management puzzle is titled "ORGANIZE"

your prospects, you are not *falling* behind. You are *already way behind!*

The good news is that you can get up to speed in a relatively short time.

There are many excellent automated systems for organizing your goals, calendar, plans and prospects. I would like to suggest if you are not already using some form of sales force automation, that you immediately visit your local computer store or talk with a business associate who is already up to speed. Do a little research and get yourself organized.

Summary

Figure 14-6 shows the essential ingredients of setting goals, planning and organizing.

Your annual goals should be driven by lifetime goals that you personally set . . . possibly with your family and other people you love. Those goals give direction to your annual business or sales goals, which should be specific and measurable.

Your annual goals drive your monthly goals. Monthly goals are fairly short term and should be typically higher

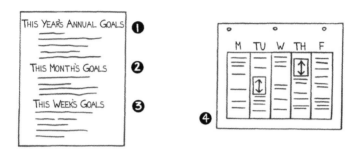

YEARLY GOALS (1) DRIVE MONTHLY GOALS (2) WHICH DRIVE YOUR
WEEKLY GOALS (3) AND YOUR WEEKLY CALENDAR (4).
THESE DRIVE YOUR DAILY SCHEDULE AND "TO-DO LIST" (5).

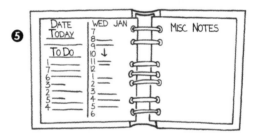

YOUR WEEKLY GOALS AND SCHEDULES DRIVE YOUR CALL GOALS (6),
WHICH ARE EVENTUALLY STORED IN YOUR ACCOUNT FOLDER (7).

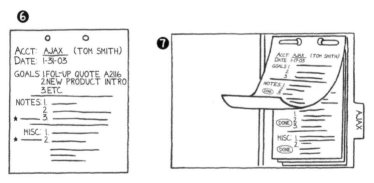

*Figure 14-6: Essential ingredients of goal setting,
planning and organization*

than one-twelfth of your yearly goals. This allows room for the unexpected (emergencies and the unknown). It also allows room for the known (competition, vacation, etc.) For example, if you were going to shoot an arrow at a distant target, you would aim higher than the bulls-eye to allow for the added influence of gravity. Similarly, if you were going to throw a ball onto the roof of a four-story building, you wouldn't aim at the top edge of the building. You would probably aim ten to twenty feet above the edge to allow for error.

Once you set your monthly goals, you break them into weekly goals and then set your calendar and daily goals.

Daily goals should consist of "to-do-list" items and planned appointments. The appointments might be with prospects, customers, coworkers or even yourself if you need a block of time for planning or completing a task. Each to-do-list item, task or appointment should move you closer to your monthly and yearly goals.

Keeping good records is also part of being organized. The best system I have seen is the one used by doctors. Their typical system is a file folder for each patient, which contains the patient's chronological medical history.

Even though your medical file can be kept in a computer, doctors still take this basic information-collecting system into the exam room because of its reliability and simplicity. I suggest you do the same for each of your prospects and customers.

It's part of being organized, and being organized is essential to being your best.

Time Management — Part 4

Remember that you don't control your time and you can't really manage it. You only manage the activities that you put into your time. If your activities are driven by organized

Natural Selling Concepts

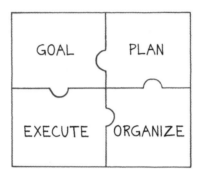

The last piece of the time management puzzle is the most important part. It's titled: "EXECUTE"

plans to accomplish significant business and personal goals, then being your best all boils down to execution.

Execution is what *Natural Selling Concepts* is all about. As stated before, all management systems must eventually degenerate into work. Your goal-setting, planning and organizing must eventually degenerate into work!

Natural Selling Concepts is a sales training program that works . . . if *you* do!

The program deals with all of the essential skills that must be mastered. Finding new business (prospecting), the first contact (the cold call), building relationships, product knowledge, finding and developing real needs, qualifying those needs, qualifying decision-makers, Up-Front Contracts, presenting, trial closing, handling objections (building and internalizing lambs), closing and following-up.

If you truly want to be your *best*, managing your goal-directed, planned and organized activities is the *best* way!

❧ CHAPTER FIFTEEN ❧
Follow-up & Thank You

Follow-up is one of those things that we all agree is critical and yet so few people actually do it. When people don't follow-up with us like we think they should, we even get angry.

There is a logical reason why it will upset you when someone doesn't follow-up with you. There's also a logical reason why you will typically not see yourself as part of the problem, even if you are.

Poor follow-up is upsetting because it's somewhere between sloppy and dishonest. It's sloppy if you're not doing what you should be doing to be your best, and it's dishonest if you're not keeping commitments. If you don't think poor follow-up is dishonest, ask yourself what it's called when someone says they'll do something, but they don't. Did they tell the truth? Or did they lie? The danger in not following-up is that what you perceive as, "Gee, I forgot," your prospect may perceive as, "Gee, he lied!"

Believing that a dropped commitment is essentially the same as lying is a good first step to being your best in following-up if it helps you develop the conviction and the commitment to become a world-class follow-upper.

You probably don't see yourself as part of the problem because, unlike your prospect, you know everything that's happening. You know all of the circumstances and you know there are reasons or excuses for not following-up. Since you know everything that you are doing all of the time, you are totally informed. This keeps you from getting angry with yourself. You have excellent follow-up with

FOLLOW-UP	BEFORE CLOSING	AFTER CLOSING
Proactive *(you initiate... your option)*	1	2
You made a commitment	3	4

Figure 15-1: Proactive Follow-Up

yourself and that's why you are so understanding of your own problems or forgetfulness. This is why you probably do not recognize your own follow-up as poor. *(Caution: It might be a blind spot.)*

There are two reasons for follow-up. First, to be proactive in the *Natural Selling Process* and second, to keep promises that you make. In addition to the two reasons for follow-up, there are two times when you need to follow-up . . . before you close . . . and after you close.

Let's look at each of the four possibilities.

1. Proactive before closing. This is the follow-up you do to move the *Natural Selling Process* forward once you have started. It is the execution phase of your planning. You plan how you are going to sell an account. You break the plan down into doable activities and you start doing them. As you implement your plan, you constantly add new activities and new follow-up steps.

Examples of this kind of follow-up include:
- calling prospects who haven't responded to your voice mails,
- following up on prospects who have not yet granted you an appointment, and
- following up with prospects who have your proposal but who have not yet made a decision, etc.

2. Proactive after closing. This follow-up is critical to insuring that you deliver as much or hopefully more than you promised.

> Examples are:
> * following up on orders to make sure all paperwork has been properly entered into your system,
> * writing thank-you notes,
> * keeping your customers informed on the status of their order, and
> * calling active customers to discuss additional products or services, etc.

3. You made a commitment to someone before the close. Whenever you tell a prospect that you "will try to get an answer" or that you "will see what you can do to get a better price," you have made a commitment. You didn't say you would do it, and you didn't say when; you only said you would try. Even so, there is a good chance your prospect interpreted that you would, and that you were going to do it right away.

I sat in on a sales call recently where the salesperson (Sam) said to a prospect, "Let me check to see if that option is available."

The prospect (Paul) said, "Fine."

I interpreted that to mean the salesperson was going to call right away and get an answer. However, Sam went on to a second subject and a short while later he ended the call and we left. Upon arriving at our car, I asked why he didn't check on the availability of the option he had mentioned. He responded that he was going to do that when he got back to his office the next day. I told him that if I was Paul, I would have been disappointed, and I would not have been impressed with that kind of delay. Sam said he knew Paul and that Paul understood that he wouldn't have the answer immediately, but that he (Sam) would have to check and get back in a day or so. I said, "Maybe that's why Paul is still a prospect and not a customer." Since I was already stepping on Sam's toes, I figured, why not go all the way, so I asked, "Do you think you missed a chance to close because you didn't have or attempt to get all of the information?"

Sam became somewhat agitated at my comment and said he would prove that Paul didn't expect an answer on the spot. Sam called Paul immediately using a cell phone with a speaker attachment in his car so I could listen. Sam asked, "Paul, were you aware that it might take a day or two to get that answer on the option we discussed, or did you expect an answer while we were with you?"

Paul responded, "Well, I was a bit surprised that you didn't have an answer and that you didn't make a call while you were here."

Sam then saved the day by asking, "If I can get the information in the next several minutes and call you right back, would you like to move forward with the project?"

Paul said, "Sure, but only if that option is available." Sam checked and immediately called back. After answering a few more of Paul's questions, he gave us the order. Sam looked at me with a sheepish grin. I didn't say a word, but arrogantly grinned back.

He said, "Oh, shut up!"

Sam learned a great lesson that day. He learned that it's not *your* perception that counts. It's the *prospect's* perception, and it's always safer to ask than to assume that you know it.

When you're making a sales call, you have to be careful to create the correct perceptions and the only way you can be sure is to ask questions and paraphrase.

It's even more important when you are closing an order because you are committing to a number of things whether you put them into writing or not. You are committing to deliver what you sold at a level of quality acceptable to your customer, on time, with no negative surprises.

It amazes me how many salespeople know this and yet still manage to drop the ball after doing all of the sales work.

Picture yourself making a major purchase (home or car) and your salesperson has committed to having the paperwork completed by Friday so you can sign. You arrive at his or her office at the appointed time on Friday and are told the salesperson is out of town on vacation. How do you feel? The normal reaction would be frustration and disappointment. Add to that the feeling that your time is not respected and that your business is obviously not important and you now have the ingredients of anger — *not* a good thing for the salesperson to generate.

You already know it's important to be honest. And you know that not keeping a commitment might be perceived as a lie. If it happens on one of the first orders you do with a prospect, you may lose more than you know. You may lose credibility, trust, and future referrals — not to mention market share and all future business with this prospect.

4. You made a commitment to someone after the close. Many salespeople believe their job is to bring the business in and the follow-up after the sale is someone else's job. Some companies even mandate this and delegate everything after the sale to their customer service department or production department, usually in the name of efficiency. However, when you close an order, you are exchanging promises with your prospect. The prospect is promising to pay for the product or service. You are promising (personally or on behalf of the company) that the product or service will be delivered on time and will meet or exceed the specifications and level of quality that were agreed upon before the sale. It is likely that you also implied (perceived by the prospect as a promise) that there would be no negative surprises.

It's okay for you to hand off a customer to other people or departments for the delivery phase of your business. However, you must be extremely careful to have a positive handoff. That's where the prospect perceives he or she is getting more service and more contacts . . . not less.

USAA in Texas is an insurance company that is especially good at this kind of follow-up. In the thirty years that they have handled my auto and homeowners insurance, I can't remember a time when I was handed off to another person without the first person giving me a good logical reason and then making sure I was okay with the transfer. When someone new comes on the telephone, they always have given me the perception that they know as much or more about me as my earlier contact. I haven't had to re-explain or repeat myself after the handoff.

Even if you do hand your new customer off to someone else in your company, you should follow-up to make sure your promises are being kept. At the very least, it's a great way to increase sales by selling add-on's, additional options, service contracts, etc. Remember from Chapter 3 on Prospecting — Your best sources of new business are your current customers. They probably don't use all of your current products or services and they're also an excellent source of referrals and new leads.

Follow Up & Thank You

So much for talking about follow-up . . . The real question is how do you do it?

The best way to be your best at follow-up is to have a system that's easy to set up and easy to maintain. Ideally, the system should encompass all (proactive or keeping commitment) follow-ups.

Each follow-up requirement starts somewhere. It may start as an action step required to accomplish a goal. It may start as a request from someone within your organization. It may start because of a commitment that you made. However it starts, there's one *best* place to collect them so they are not lost or forgotten.

The system I am going to show you is easy to set up. It's easy to use. And you don't have to buy special software or materials to use it. All you need is a pad of paper and something to write with.

The easiest way to picture the system is to think about the medical record that your doctor uses to document your health. It's a chronological journal of your health history in a paper folder. It might also contain x-rays, reminders, test results and information relating to your specific condition.

Whenever the doctor wants to note an action item, a star (☆) is placed in the left margin to designate that "action is needed." The folder is not re-filed until all noted action items are:

(a) completed,

(b) transferred to a calendar, or

(c) transferred to someone's to-do list. Then, when the folder is re-filed, a follow-up date is also noted on the doctor's calendar for your next visit.

Now, consider a similar system for tracking your own promises, commitments and required follow-ups.

Natural Selling Concepts

Remember, the star (☆) is the key. Wherever you put a star, you have a follow-up required.

The next two illustrations are examples of planning and follow-up pages that you should have in your records. Figure 15-2 shows a weekly planning guide and Figure 15-3 shows a typical page of notes from sales calls and telephone calls.

You can custom develop forms if you want and enter your notes electronically, but hand-written on plain paper is preferred and typically more convenient.

The example shown in Figure 15-3 has notes from several different kinds of activity. It's best to use a separate sheet of paper for each prospect, customer, meeting, etc.

Now, let's review what you need to do to be your best.

First, identify your proactive follow-up requirements. Take your annual goals and break them into "bite-sized action steps." These action steps are actually the follow-up steps that you must take to accomplish your goals. Each action step should be preceded by a ☆ and a blank space "_____". The purpose of the blank space is to remind you to move the commitment (action step) into your calendar or to-do list. After you complete the action step, plan it on your calendar or note it on your to-do list, you should immediately fill in the blank with "<u>DONE</u>" or "<u>XFER</u>" (transferred). As soon as all of the blanks are filled, indicating that you have completed or planned all action steps, file the sheet of paper into the appropriate storage file (prospect, product, goals, personal, etc.).

Second, use this same system to record and manage your daily notes and activities. Follow the same rules for completing your action steps and filing these sheets for future reference. Reminder . . . It's *best* to use a separate sheet of paper for each prospect, customer, supplier, meeting, etc. This makes the subsequent filing (once all blanks are filled in) much simpler.

WEEKLY PLANNING GUIDE

REVIEW YOUR GOALS EACH WEEK AND DECIDE WHICH ACTION STEPS TO TAKE. KEEP THIS SHEET IN YOUR ACTIVE FOLDER *UNTIL ALL* ACTION ITEMS HAVE BEEN ACCOMPLISHED, NOTED ON YOUR CALENDAR, OR NOTED ON YOUR TO-DO LIST.

ANNUAL GOALS... REVIEW YOUR MONTHLY GOALS ONCE PER MONTH AND NOTE WHICH ACTION STEPS YOU SHOULD TAKE THIS MONTH

- ✸ $2 MILLION IN NEW SALES
- ✸ $5 MILLION IN REPEAT SALES
- ✸ 10 NEW ACCOUNTS

MONTHLY GOALS... REVIEW YOUR MONTHLY GOALS ONCE PER WEEK AND NOTE WHICH ACTIONS STEPS YOU SHOULD TAKE THIS WEEK

- ✸ $200K IN NEW SALES AND $500K IN REPEAT SALES
- ✸ 1 NEW ACCOUNT SIGNED UP
- ✸ ATTEND STELLAR SALES TRAINING SEMINAR
- ✸ _____

WEEKLY GOALS... REVIEW YOUR WEEKLY GOALS EACH DAY AND NOTE WHICH ACTION STEPS YOU SHOULD TAKE DAILY

- ✸ 12 SALES CALLS ON EXISTING ACCOUNTS
- ✸ 8 SALES CALLS ON NEW PROSPECT ACCOUNTS
- ✸ _____

DAILY GOALS... SET AND *DO* DAILY GOALS

- ✸ 10 TELEPHONE CALLS TO PROSPECT ACCOUNTS
- ✸ 5 FACE-TO-FACE SALES CALLS
- ✸ _____

Figure 15-2: Weekly Planning Guide

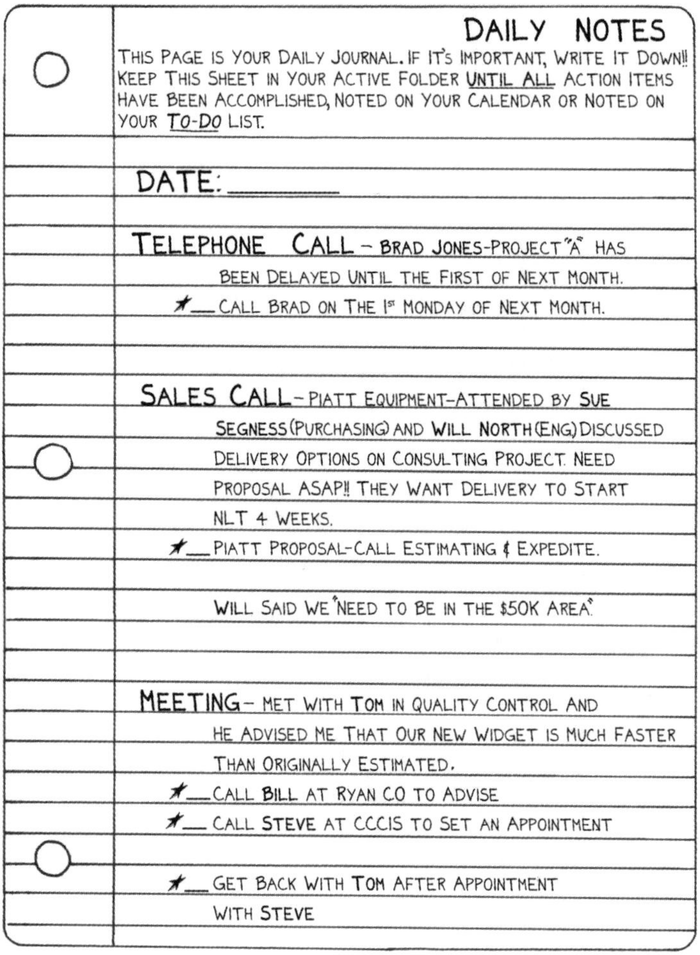

DAILY NOTES

THIS PAGE IS YOUR DAILY JOURNAL. IF IT'S IMPORTANT, WRITE IT DOWN!! KEEP THIS SHEET IN YOUR ACTIVE FOLDER <u>UNTIL ALL</u> ACTION ITEMS HAVE BEEN ACCOMPLISHED, NOTED ON YOUR CALENDAR OR NOTED ON YOUR <u>TO-DO</u> LIST.

DATE: _____

TELEPHONE CALL – BRAD JONES-PROJECT "A" HAS
BEEN DELAYED UNTIL THE FIRST OF NEXT MONTH.
✱___ CALL BRAD ON THE 1ˢᵗ MONDAY OF NEXT MONTH.

SALES CALL – PIATT EQUIPMENT-ATTENDED BY SUE
SEGNESS (PURCHASING) AND WILL NORTH (ENG) DISCUSSED
DELIVERY OPTIONS ON CONSULTING PROJECT. NEED
PROPOSAL ASAP!! THEY WANT DELIVERY TO START
NLT 4 WEEKS.
✱___ PIATT PROPOSAL-CALL ESTIMATING & EXPEDITE.

WILL SAID WE NEED TO BE IN THE $50K AREA.

MEETING – MET WITH TOM IN QUALITY CONTROL AND
HE ADVISED ME THAT OUR NEW WIDGET IS MUCH FASTER
THAN ORIGINALLY ESTIMATED.
✱___ CALL BILL AT RYAN CO TO ADVISE
✱___ CALL STEVE AT CCCIS TO SET AN APPOINTMENT

✱___ GET BACK WITH TOM AFTER APPOINTMENT
WITH STEVE

Figure 15-3:
Daily Notes & Commitments

The system we just defined is incredibly simple. If you follow it carefully, all of your follow-up requirements will be in your pad-folder until they are completed or transferred to a calendar or to-do list. Your customer files will contain a complete history of past action steps and notes just like your doctor's file contains your complete medical history.

You now have the system. All you need is the resolve and the decision to do it. As you work the system, you will have confidence that you are being your best for yourself, for your company and for your prospects and customers.

Before we leave this chapter, several other follow-up systems are worthy of mention...

1. **Pre-order checklist** — Develop a checklist to remind yourself of each critical step in the *Natural Selling Process* in addition to your company's order entry process. If your company does not provide an order-entry checklist, assume responsibility to develop your own.

2. **Post-order checklist** — Develop a checklist to remind yourself of each critical step that you should take (especially including follow-up) after an order or contract is entered. Again, if your company does not provide a post-order checklist, assume responsibility to develop your own.

Natural Selling Concept #29

Follow-up is the bridge between you and your prospect. It can significantly accelerate the relationship-building process when done properly. Confirming details in writing as soon as possible is the best way to improve communication and lower the possibility of misunderstanding.

Natural Selling Concepts

Let's look at a couple of specific problems that can be greatly reduced by a good post-order checklist . . .

a) **Buyer's Remorse** — This is when your decision-maker changes his mind. It usually only happens when the decision-maker is spending his own money.

Buyer's remorse is the regret that sets in as soon as the buyer's memory of value becomes less vivid and less exciting than their memory of cost.

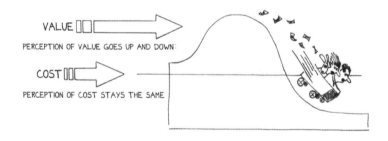

Figure 15-4: Value, Cost, Perception

How do you prevent it?

The same way you should follow-up on every critical order — take immediate *action,* have your prospect initial or sign the agreement, then, schedule periodic follow-ups to review and reinforce the benefits that your product or service provided. And, above all, only sell "honest" needs. *(Refer back to our definition of selling — Only fill needs where you and your prospect both make a profit or gain.)*

b)   **Order Cancellations and Change Orders** — It
would be nice if you could prevent them, but you
can't. You can greatly reduce them by communicating accurately and confirming details clearly in
writing, but you will probably never eliminate
them. Why? Because prospects and customers
sometimes change their minds and sometimes
situations change that force prospects to make
changes or cancellations.

We can't eliminate them, but we can decide
ahead of time what strategy to employ when they
do happen.

The best approach I know is to assume they're
legitimate constraints. Probe to get all of the
details and go back to the Up-Front Contract. If
they are not legitimate constraints, treat them like
delayed objections, probe and question until you
can go for a new Up-Front Contract.

If you get them regularly, build a lamb or start
addressing them earlier in the sales process, prefer-
ably in the *Identify Need* block *(Fig. 2-1 and
Chapter 7)* . . . no later than the *Presentation* block
(Fig. 2-1 and Chapter 9).

Good follow-up is critical . . . An appropriate "thank
you" is the best postscript to every call.

Unfortunately, the common thank you is so overused
that it has lost much of its impact. It's especially annoying
to hear salespeople say, "Thanks for your time." Think
about it! What does "Thank you for your time" do? First,
it reminds the other person that you have used something
of theirs that they don't have enough of already. Second, it

communicates that their time was more valuable than yours. Have you ever felt really uplifted when someone thanked you for your time? Or, do you feel a bit down having been reminded that you now have less of it?

It's much better to sincerely thank a person for something that will lift them up.

How about . . .

"Thank you for meeting with me; I appreciate your courtesy and professionalism."

"Thanks for a great meeting; your input is going to make a great difference in _____."

"Thank you for trusting us with your business; you are going to be pleased with our delivery and service."

"Thanks for explaining your situation; your input is going to save time for both of us."

"I really appreciate your positive attitude . . . It's a real pleasure doing business with you."

In conclusion, there are millions of ways to say thank you, but there's only one best. That best will be determined by your situation and the person you are thanking. If you want it to be best, make it honest, sincere and uplifting. Never make it routine or trite.

One last word about follow-up and thank you: A great technique is to write a short thank-you card and leave it with the receptionist on your way out of an important appointment. It will probably be delivered a short while later and will be a great reminder that you are a professional. You might even consider having special cards printed for such occasions.

CHAPTER SIXTEEN

Continuing to Grow . . .
Suggested Reading

The last step in *Natural Selling Concepts* is putting it to work. Before you do that, there's one other thing you should do. Set a personal goal to become an avid reader. There are hundreds of excellent books. Set a goal to read one per week or one per month. If you are not a disciplined reader, set a goal to read at least one book . . . and then another.

Early in my career, a friend suggested to me that, "Reading may not learn ya nothin', but it won't dumb you up!" He was right. The books I have listed in this chapter are the best I have read. There are many other newer books, but I'm recommending these for you because they are timeless and they are classics.

Principles don't change. Four thousand years ago, Solomon wrote, " . . . there is nothing new under the sun." He was saying that all of the principles have already been discovered. However, times and cultures change and in this new part of history, you must study to understand and apply those principles to your life if you want to be your best.

Suggested reading list:
1. *How I Raised Myself from Failure to Success in Selling* by Frank Bettger — You can find this one on our web page: www.B-Elite.com. This is without a doubt the best book ever written on sales!
2. *Secrets of Closing Sales* by Charles Roth — This is an all-time classic. Some of the techniques are "Websterish." Read this book and ignore the Webster

techniques. The balance will be worth the investment in your time.

3. *The Greatest Salesman in the World* by Og Mandino — This is the all-time #1 Best Seller in sales motivation. I doubt that a better book will ever be written in the area of sales motivation. A few years back, I had the honor of personally meeting Og Mandino. He said, *The Greatest Salesman in the World* had become so popular that a "first-edition" copy of the book is now valued at over $500, more if signed. The value has probably gone up even more since the book was subsequently translated into Japanese and became a best seller in Japan. Og Mandino wrote a sequel to *The Greatest Salesman in the World* and has written a number of other excellent motivational and entertaining books. Next to Horatio Alger, Og Mandino is my favorite author.

4. *How to Get Control of Your Time and Your Life* by Alan Lakein — This is an excellent book on time management. Actually, it's an excellent book on how to manage the activities you put into the time you have.

5. *Hand Me Another Brick* by Charles Swindoll — This is an excellent book on basic management technique.

6. *Man's Search for Meaning* by Victor Frankl — This book is especially good when considering personal goals.

7. *Focus* by Al Reis — You can only do one thing at a time and you can only be as effective as your focus will allow. This book is especially good when considering prioritization of goals.

8. *Selling: Principles and Practices* by Russel, Beach and

Buskirk. Most trade books focus on one aspect of selling like motivation or planning or closing. This book is a college textbook that covers many other aspects of selling that are not covered in trade books. It is especially good for an overall view of the way selling fits into the marketing process.

9. *Life is Tremendous* by Charles E. Jones — Excellent book for motivation and for maintaining a "right" attitude. Charlie Jones is so dynamic and motivated that he has come to be known as Charlie "Tremendous" Jones.

10. *See You at the Top* by Zig Zigler — This is another tremendous motivational book written especially from a salesperson's perspective.

11. *The Best Seller* by D. Forbes Ley — This book almost attempts to deliver too much. It is a good resource, like the text mentioned earlier, that covers many aspects of professional selling.

12. *The 22 Immutable Laws of Marketing* by Al Ries and Jack Trout — This is a great book for salespeople who need to understand more about marketing and for marketing people who need to understand more about sales. The discipline of marketing is actually a compilation of three more focused disciplines: sales, advertising/promotion and research. This book blows away much of the smoke that marketers use to over-complicate marketing.

13. *How to Sell More in Less Time with No Rejection* by Art Sobczak — This book would be more accurately titled, "Less Rejection." Nothing works all of the time! It is an excellent resource for people who primarily sell on the telephone. Be cautious to weed out the Webster

techniques as you glean the nuggets of wisdom. Also, this book might still be self-published and the best way to obtain a copy may be to search the Internet.

14. *The Book of Proverbs in the Bible* — Often referred to as the "Book of Wisdom." Read it and you will know why. In thirty-one short chapters, you will be exposed to some of the greatest sales, management and personal advice that is available anywhere.

15. *Selling the Invisible* by Harry Bechwith — This book tends to focus on selling intangibles. However, it has many great principles and insights into the sales process for selling tangibles too.

NATURAL SELLING CONCEPT #30

"If you do not read, you are no better off than someone who can't read."

— Charles "Tremendous" Jones

Let me repeat what I said earlier: There are hundreds of excellent books. Set a goal to read one per week or one per month. If you are not a disciplined reader, set a goal to read at least one book . . . and then another.

As far as habits are concerned, it's probably one of the best you can develop in your quest to become your best.

Now you're ready to put *Natural Selling Concepts* to work!

❦ CHAPTER SEVENTEEN ❦
Putting *Natural Selling Concepts* to Work

Now that you have completed reading *Natural Selling Concepts*, I hope you will agree that it's the most straightforward and common-sense approach to selling that you have ever seen.

There are eight things you need to do to make *Natural Selling Concepts* work. Do these eight things and you'll be well on your way to being your best.

1. Decide how to best describe what you sell and develop your Five-Point Presentation.

(Ref. Chapter 3, in the section titled: "What are the best sources of new business?") You need to be able to describe what you do well enough that a fifteen-year-old would be able to understand, remember, *and* be able to repeat it to others. Write it down and use it as the header for your Five-Point Presentation sheet.

Then, decide what the five most important things are that you sell and develop a one-page presentation.

The five things must be specific. "Sell cars" is specific; "Sell electronic components" is specific; "Sell memberships" is specific; "Sell health insurance" is specific. However, "Sell quality" is not specific; and "Sell our service" is not specific. Remember, listeners must understand and mentally picture exactly what you are selling and see in their "mind's eye" how it will benefit them more than the cost, or they will never buy!

You don't *have* to do this. If you don't have a best way to describe what you sell and you don't have a five-point presentation, it will not make you worse. You just will not be able to consistently make your best presentation.

2. Develop your elevator speeches.

(Ref. Chapter 4) There are seven occurrences where an elevator speech will benefit you. Six are used with first contacts and the seventh is used with someone you already know.

a. *Receptionist.* Ask for help with names.

b. *Secretary or assistant.* Be ready to tell what you do in broad general terms and be ready with a logical reason why they "should put you through."

c. *Voice mail or recorder.* Be ready with the seven-step approach to give a compelling reason for the prospect to call back.

d. *Voice to voice.* Similar to a voice mail elevator speech but shorter and more personal. Be sure to end every sentence and every answer with a request for a face-to-face in-person appointment or for a voice-to-voice telephone appointment.

e. *Objections to going forward.* Remember there are only two responses to a request for an appointment. One is an objection; one is not!

You will hear either, "This is not a good time," which is not an objection, it only means you need to offer a second or third time to set the appointment, or you will hear, "I don't want to waste time," which is an objection. Keep in mind, there are millions of ways for your prospect to say, "I don't want to waste time." Typical examples include: "We're happy with our current supplier," "We already have a contract," "We're not approving new vendors," etc.

Remember, if the prospect asks you to "send something," a good lamb might be, "We can bury you with literature . . . but it might be quicker to get together to have a look." If they say, "Tell me more about it," a good lamb might be, "It would probably take less time in person than on the telephone. How about (second date or time) if (first date or time) aren't good?"

One other reminder: If you want to pre-qualify the prospect before making the first in-person sales call, you might open a dialog by saying, "I would like to ask you a couple of questions to make sure you're the correct person for me to be calling on." Then, ask for the appointment after you are sure that you have the right person.

f. *First face-to-face or voice-to-voice appointment.* There really is only one best way to do a first call. It starts with a quick thank you and introduction and then immediately goes into, "There are three goals to accomplish during our time together.

"First, I would like to tell you a little about who we are and what we do and how we're different. Then, I would like to find out more about you and your company goals as they relate to what we do. And third, I'd like to see if there are some ways that we might support you in accomplishing your goals."

Then proceed with the call as outlined in Chapter 5.

g. *All subsequent calls.* Basically, they follow the same pattern. "I appreciate meeting with you today and I have four things on my list . . . I have three goals for today . . . You wanted to go over some recent order details and then if we have time, I would like discuss two other issues." All of these are variations of the same approach.

Remember to be brief, bright and gone in every call. Brief, bright and gone doesn't mean quick, smart and abrupt! It means productive and to the point with accuracy and intelligence without overstaying your welcome.

If you don't develop elevator speeches, you can continue to "wing it" and you will continue to succeed at your current rate. It will not make you worse. You just will not be able to consistently do your best!

3. Build your question inventory.

(Ref. Chapter 7, in the section titled: "How do you improve your ability to ask questions?") Determine the types of decision-makers you call on and then develop a list of best questions for each type. Some questions will be on each list and some will be specific to only one type of decision-maker.

If you are selling a technical product, you will need a list of good questions for engineering, purchasing and management people. If you are selling a service to consumers, you may need lists for husbands, wives, couples, singles, male heads of households and female heads of households.

If you don't build an inventory of best questions to ask, you will not be able to consistently discover the needs of the prospects and customers you call on. If you don't do your best at finding their real needs, guess what? That's right! It will not make you worse, you just will not make your best presentation. In fact, you may not get to make a presentation at all!

4. Construct your lambs.

(Ref. Chapter 11). There are only eight kinds of objections. They aren't inventing new ones. So, if you know the objections and you know you are going to hear them again and again, then you need to go into every call with a memorized (complete) list of best answers (lambs) to your prospect's objections.

- Develop your list of objections.
- Develop best responses to each.
- Commit these to memory so you can be natural and flexible when you're under pressure.
- Get closer to more orders.
- Close more orders.

More good news! If you don't develop your list of lambs and have them ready, it will not make you worse. You just will not be able to consistently have the best response available when it really counts. Any guess what that will do to your closing percentage?

5. Decide how you are going to close.

(Ref. Chapter 12) There are only so many ways you can ask for an order. There may be millions of variations, but the basic list is fairly short. You can rename them if that makes you more comfortable, but you have to use them if you want to do your best.

Buyers aren't wired to reject you; they're wired to object. They aren't wired to buy; they're wired to wait. That's why you need to close. You need to precipitate action. If you're not closing, if you're not precipitating some action, you're just visiting. Visiting doesn't pay as well as closing.

If you don't decide ahead of time when and how you are going to close and what you are going to say, you will not consistently use your *best* way to close. You may be awesome, but you will only be your *best* (awesomest) if you know when and how to close and if you're ready with the *best* way.

6. Personalize your "Quality Card."

(Reference: Chapter 13) If you don't measure something, you can't manage it. If you are not somehow measuring your quality, then you are guessing about how good you really are. And, since blind spots are impossible to see, you can't possibly accurately measure your quality without the help of an outside source.

Your best outside sources are your coworkers, your managers and your subordinates. Each of them has a different perspective than you. If they see something that they think is good or bad, it's important for you to know because if they see it, maybe your prospects and decision-makers are also seeing it.

You don't *have* to measure your quality. You can go through a complete career without ever knowing how good (or how bad) you really are. If you don't measure your quality, it will not make you worse. It will, however, inhibit you from being your best. After all, if you have no objective feedback, you have no basis for change. No change means no improvement.

7. Determine what company goals you need to accomplish.

(Reference: Chapter 14) Whether you work for yourself or for an international corporation, you are working to

accomplish goals. You must have a clear understanding of those goals; otherwise it's impossible to be motivated or to have a good attitude. It's also impossible to have fun if you don't know where the "finish line" is.

The best goals follow certain fundamental guidelines. They are written, specific (clear enough to be visualized), measurable, stretching (but realistic and achievable), and time-framed. A good goal will have two time constraints. One is a specific deadline and the other is always, "As soon as possible!"

If you don't have company goals, it will not make you worse. You just will not achieve your best! How can you hit a target that you cannot see?

8. Clearly specify (in writing) your personal goals well enough that, in your mind's eye, you can see them accomplished.

The only reason people go to work for a company is to accomplish personal goals. If they see that they are accomplishing these goals, they will never leave the company unless they are forced out (fired, promoted, retire or die) or if they perceive that they can better accomplish their personal goals somewhere else. Personal goals are the key to success in any endeavor. Personal goals are the reason you start working, they're the reason you stop and they're the reason you do your best in between.

If you don't have personal goals, you cannot be your best. The stronger they are, the more motivated you will be. The stronger they are, the better the chances you will have a great attitude. The more clearly defined they are, the more fun you will have achieving them! Not having personal goals will not make you worse. You just will not be able to consistently do your best!

Natural Selling Concepts

A little something extra . . .

This book has been all about being your *best*.

Now, I would like to share how the principles that guided this book have had a major impact on me personally. Before I do, I want to caution you. These principles are based on principles from the Bible.

Some people find the Bible offensive. I assure you I do not want in any way to offend you. However, the Bible was given to us by God and it explains how to have your best life. Part of having your best life means doing and being your best. This means developing discipline while avoiding non-productive behavior. God's Word lists many principles that clearly define right and wrong behavior.

Some people are currently involved in lifestyles and behaviors that violate Scriptural principles. These people have what might be called spiritual blind spots. If you are willing to be open to the possibility that you might have some of these blind spots, please read on. If you are not open or do not believe in the Bible as a book from God, but you are willing to have an open mind to hear what God's Word (in the Bible) did in my life, then I challenge you to read the last chapter. Please read it with an open mind. It's like a testimony in a court of law. It's not designed to tell you what to believe and it's not meant to condemn you in any way. It is my story and as clearly as possible describes what happened in my life and why I am so sure that it is the best.

I encourage you to read it carefully and ask yourself if the same principles that changed my life might apply to you also.

AFTERWORD

When I started writing *Natural Selling Concepts*, it was my desire that all of the principles and techniques that I used would be based on the principles of the Bible. To the best of my ability, I believe this has been accomplished.

The goal in this "personal application" is to show you how these principles have impacted my life as well as this book.

Natural Selling Concepts has been a step-by-step approach to the selling process. It started with prospecting, then cold calling, establishing rapport, etc. Now I would like to go through those same steps to show you how the principles impacted me.

I'm going to assume that we've already hit the first two steps (prospecting and cold calling) and we have also established a little bit of rapport. Hopefully, you realize I'm a fairly normal kind of a person. I don't have two heads. I'm not a person who tries to force my beliefs on someone else. I don't care for people who would use the Bible to force their beliefs on me so I certainly don't want to do that to you.

The courtroom is a good metaphor to help explain my intent in this chapter.

In a criminal court of law, you typically have the following:

1. Defense attorney

2. Prosecuting attorney

3. Judge

4. Jury

5. Gallery

6. Witnesses

7. Court reporter

Natural Selling Concepts

The function of the witness is to testify to what they have seen and know and what they can prove as fact. The function of the court reporter is to record things exactly as they are said and exactly as they happen.

My objective is to be a witness to you and to report things from my life exactly as they happened.

I was born in 1946 and lived in West Virginia until I was around fourteen years old. Then my family moved to Florida and we lived there until I was nineteen years old. I worked at Kennedy Space Center while I went to college and got a degree in electrical engineering. Then I joined the Air Force during the Viet Nam era and ended up as a pilot spending my tour of duty in Germany.

When I got out of the Air Force, I came to Dayton, Ohio, to work for an electronic parts distributor. I worked in inside sales for a while, then went to outside sales. After that, I went to work for Texas Instruments in Los Angeles and sold consumer products. After a short but successful career in consumer sales, I was offered a management position for another electronics parts distributor and ended up moving back to Ohio.

So I worked a lot of different places, and you might think at this point that I just couldn't hold a job. And maybe that was partly true. I also couldn't hold a family together because it had fallen apart. At that point, I just hadn't grown up. Unlike a lot of people who have their families fall apart, I couldn't blame the other person. I had to blame myself. I knew down inside that it was really my fault. Yet I didn't know what I had done wrong. You might say that I was on a kind of spiritual quest, trying to find out what the purpose of life was, why I would do certain things, why other things I did didn't make sense and yet I would do them anyway. So you could say I was definitely looking for answers in my life. I was in my late twenties and was divorced. My ex-wife had remarried, I had two sons whom I loved who were now living in California — and I was in Ohio. So you can see my life was in a bit of a mess.

That's when I started really wondering about the purpose of life.

I started to look around at various options to satisfy this curiosity, and I don't have to tell you there are some pretty weird beliefs and religions out there!

I figured that if there really was a God, He probably would make a lot more sense than most members of these weird religions. So I just kept looking — I looked at different types of religions, I looked at some that were considered cults, I looked at everything I could find. I looked at Protestantism, Catholicism, Unitarianism and Humanism . . . I looked at different denominations and very little made sense until one day a person challenged me. He asked, "Carl, you consider yourself a fairly intelligent person, don't you?"

Well, I couldn't argue with that! So I said, "Of course I consider myself fairly intelligent."

Then he asked, "How can you argue against something that you've never really looked at . . . something you have never really read?"

I answered, "Well, I've read the Bible."

He asked, "Which part are you having trouble with?"

I answered, "It's full of inconsistencies and there are a lot of other things about the Bible that I don't necessarily agree with."

So he said, "Let's look at them," and then he actually volunteered to help me go through some of these things. What he really had done was call my bluff because I had not actually read that much of the Bible.

That's when he said, "Look, if you're as intelligent as I think you are, you really should get in and prove for yourself whether those concepts and principles in the Bible are true or false."

Later that day when I was by myself, I said a little prayer. I said, "God, if you're real, then surely you can show yourself to me, and if you're not real, then I'm going to find that out, too. But one way or the other I'm going to get this thing behind me."

Truthfully, I was really thinking more of getting it behind me than believing.

So I started looking into the Bible, and what I found really hurt a lot. The reason it hurt was because I started finding principles that I had violated. Every principle that I violated had caused major consequences in my life. Every major consequence in my life, it seemed, came about because I had violated one or more of these Biblical principles! I still had some troubles with the Bible. I still thought it had inconsistencies, but I couldn't find them! The more I looked in the Bible, the more I realized its principles and concepts were true. It really did have a lot of good stuff for living today.

I also realized at this time of my life that my children were growing up without me, and so you might say that I was in the sales process right at the stage where I had identified a real need.

It was becoming obvious that I needed to get my life in order. A solid foundation was needed, one that was logical and could be proven to be true in my own life. So I started studying the Bible.

The first step was identifying a need. I identified the need that I had to get my life straightened out, and I started looking for answers. The more I looked in the

Bible, the more I realized that this wasn't just another how-to book with a lot of hair-brained ideas. It was really a book that had some good concepts and principles that I could live by. So I started to practice these principles and I discovered whenever I practiced a principle that was in the Bible, I found the principle was true! And whenever I violated one, there was a consequence. It was amazing!

One time a Christian friend asked me, "If Babe Ruth were to come back to life and someone were to say that he was going to get 3,000 hits in a row, would you believe it?"

And of course, I said, "No way! Nobody would ever get 3,000 hits in a row!" It's hard enough to get 3,000 hits in a career . . . much less in a row!

He said, "So you'd bet money that Babe Ruth wouldn't do it?"

And I said, "Sure."

Then he said, "Well, what about if he had already gotten 1,000 of them in a row? Would you now bet money that he wouldn't get 3,000?"

And I said to myself, *Well, I still don't think he could get 2,000 more but it's getting a little scary.*

Then he said, "What if he had 2,000 in a row and now he was getting up to bat. Would you bet that on the next at bat he wouldn't get a hit?"

And I said, "Of course not! If he already had 2,000 in a row, I'm not going to bet against him on the next one."

Then he said, "There are probably 3,000 to 4,000 predictions and promises in the Bible. To this day, every one of them has come true! And there are other things in the Bible — principles, promises and guidelines. If you don't follow them, there will come a time in your life when you will have a consequence."

So I thought, *Well, if that's the case, I'd better study this*

Natural Selling Concepts

a bit more!

I started in the Old Testament and I studied the Book of Proverbs. Some people call Proverbs "The Book of Wisdom." I found some very interesting principles that I subsequently used to build *Natural Selling Concepts.*

I would like to share a few of those with you here.

As you look at the following principles from the Bible, apply them to sales and ask yourself if the Bible is applicable.

I have listed some verses from Proverbs, but there are literally thousands of principle-defining verses in the Bible. All of the following are from the Book of Proverbs. It's the twentieth book in the Bible. There are sixty-six books in the Bible. Each one has wisdom and principles that apply to business as well as personal life. (When you see "Prov. 29:20," it means the reference is from the book of Proverbs in the 29th chapter and in the 20th verse.) All of the verses below are quoted from the *New International Version* of the Bible.

1. Prov. 5:10 — *"A little sleep, a little slumber, a little folding of the hands to rest — and poverty will come on you like a bandit and scarcity like an armed man."* This sounds like activity multiplied by quality yields results.

2. Prov. 10:5 — *"He who gathers crops in summer is a wise son, but he who sleeps during harvest is a disgraceful son."*

3. Prov. 10:8 — *"The wise in heart accept commands, but a chattering fool comes to ruin."*

4. Prov. 10:19 — *"When words are many, sin is not absent, but he who holds his tongue is wise."* Sound like you should maybe talk less than half the time?

5. Prov. 10:24 — *"What the wicked dreads will overtake him. What the righteous desire will be granted."* One way or the other, good or bad, you will get what you

deserve.

6. Prov. 11:14 — *"For lack of guidance a nation falls, but many advisors make victory sure."*

7. Prov. 12:24 — *"Diligent hands will rule; but laziness ends in slave labor."*

8. Prov. 13:3 — *"He who guards his lips guards his soul, but the one who speaks rashly will come to ruin."*

9. Prov. 13:10 — *"Pride only breeds quarrels, but wisdom is found in those who take advice."*

10. Prov. 14:23 — *"All hard work brings a profit, but mere talk leads only to poverty."* Managers love that one.

11. Prov. 15:19 — *"The way of the sluggard is blocked with thorns, but the path of the upright is a high way."*

12. Prov. 15:22 — *"Plans fail for lack of counsel, but with many advisors they succeed."* One of your best advisors is going to be your sales manager. He or she has lots of advice, but it's easy to think that you should know it all. It's good to ask for advice.

13. Prov. 17:28 — This was quoted back in Chapter 7. It was written 4,000 years ago by Solomon. *"Even a fool is thought wise if he keeps silent, and discerning if he holds his tongue."* Some people think Abraham Lincoln originated it. You may have heard it quoted, "Better to be silent and thought a fool than open your mouth and remove all doubt!"

14. Prov. 18:2 — *"A fool finds no pleasure in understanding but delights in airing his own opinions."*

15. Prov. 18:9 — *"One who is slack in his work is brother to one who destroys."* We cannot be slack; we've got to work hard; we've got to be diligent.

16. Prov. 18:13 — *"He who answers before listening — that*

is his folly and his shame."

17. Prov. 19:20 — *"Listen to advice and accept instruction and in the end you'll be wise."*

18. Prov. 21:23 — *"He who guards his mouth and his tongue keeps himself from calamity."*

19. Prov. 22:1 — *"A good name is more desirable than great riches, and to be esteemed is better than silver or gold."* Webster selling is wrong! Talk to anybody who's retired . . . talk to anybody who's been selling for many years and they'll tell you there's a lot of truth in this principle. A good name really is more desirable than great riches.

20. Prov. 25:15 — *"Through patience a ruler can be persuaded and a gentle tongue can break a bone."* You may know some buyers you would like to try that on!

21. Prov. 25:17 — *"Seldom set foot in your neighbor's house. Too much of you and he will hate you."* This sounds like, "Be brief, be bright and be gone."

22. Prov. 26:14 — *"As a door turns on its hinges, so the sluggard turns in his bed."* Work harder and smarter!

23. Prov. 27:12 — *"The prudent see danger and take refuge, but the simple keep going and suffer for it."* Planning is a critical part of business.

24. Prov. 27:17 — *"As iron sharpens iron, so one man sharpens another."* We called that "3rd party feed-back" in *Natural Selling Concept #28.*

25. Prov. 29:20 — *"Do you see a man who speaks in haste? There is more hope for a fool than him."* Sounds like asking questions and learning might be better than talking about yourself.

When I first read these things, I knew . . . if the Bible

has this kind of wisdom in just one of the sixty-six books, maybe I should check out the rest of it. So I started reading the whole Bible, not just Proverbs. The more I read, the more I was able to recognize the principles at work in my own life. I knew from my own experience that these principles were accurate and they really did work!

At that particular point I was developing an insatiable appetite to get wisdom — to learn what the Bible really had to say, and to learn its concepts and principles. I wanted to live my life following these principles, because I was pretty tired of making mistakes . . . of living my life in a way that created major negative consequences.

I had identified, you might say, a major need.

The next step after identifying a need in the sales process was an Up-Front Contract, and I was a little shocked to find out that God had an Up-Front Contract in the Bible!

He had written it there. He had said in the book of Deuteronomy, Chapter 4, verse 29, *"Those who seek me will find me."* God had already made the Up-Front Contract and I was already seeking Him, so He was promising that I would find Him!

The more I read, the more I found that there were certain laws. These weren't just principles! They were laws. And if you violate a law, you pay a price.

If you jump off a ten-story building, as one man said, "You ain't going sideways!" There's a law of gravity that takes over just as soon as you're in the air and that law will not be violated. If you try to violate it, there's a good chance you're going to suffer a major negative consequence! Well, I learned that God also has spiritual laws in the Bible, and some of those laws initially frightened me. I'd like to share some of those laws with you.

Natural Selling Concepts

The first law is that God loves you and has a wonderful plan for your life. Just as we establish laws to protect our children (e.g. no alcohol, cigarettes, or driving privileges until our children reach a certain age), God establishes laws to protect us and keep us safe for the "best" things He wants us to have. In John 3:16, it says, *"For God so loved the world that he gave his one and only Son, that whoever believes in him shall not perish but have eternal life."* Jesus then said in John 10:10b, *"I have come that they may have life, and have it to the full."* In other words, Jesus came that life might be full and meaningful. And that's what I needed! I needed a full and meaningful life.

The second law is that man was sinful and separated from God, and therefore he couldn't know and experience God's love and plan for his life. It says in Romans 3:23, *"For all have sinned and come short of the glory of God."* I knew that I had sinned, I knew I had done wrong and I knew I had hurt people. I was genuinely sorry for it but I didn't really know what I could do about it. It says in the Bible, Romans 6:23a, *"The wages of sin is death."* And that is eternal separation from God, spending an eternity away from God, and I didn't want that. I definitely had a need!

The third law is that Jesus Christ is God's only provision for man's sin. John 14:6 quotes Jesus as saying, *"I am the way and the truth and the life. No one comes to the Father except through me."*

That was a little harder for me to accept because I thought there's got to be a lot of different ways to heaven.

Everything else I had seen in the Bible so far I could prove as being true. So when I came across this verse, it was pretty hard for me. I thought, *"I've done some pretty good things, and they should count for something."* But according to John 14:6, they didn't!

Afterword

The fourth law said that I had to individually receive Christ as my Savior and Lord. John 1:12, said, *"Yet to all who received him, to those who believed in his name, he gave the right to become children of God."* In Ephesians 2:8 & 9 it says, *"For it is by grace you have been saved, through faith — and this not from yourselves, it is the gift of God — not by works, so that no one can boast."*

Well, at that point in my life I had already proven that most everything else didn't work, and I had gotten to the point where I knew that God was my last hope. He should have been my first hope, but I came to realize that He was my only hope!

Now I realized that I had gone past the "identify the need" phase and through the Up-Front Contract phase where God had said, *"I love those who love me, and those who seek me find me."* Prov. 8:17.

I had also gone through the presentation phase — I knew God loved me and had a plan for me. I knew that in my heart. I knew I was sinful and separated from Him. I really did believe that Christ was the only way. But I still had a few objections.

My biggest objection was giving up things in my life that Christians seemed to think were bad. I really didn't want to give anything up, except maybe my problems.

Then a thought came to me. If I were to go to a five-year-old boy who was playing in a mud puddle and tell him he won't want to play in mud puddles when he grows up, he would probably say "No way! I like playing in mud puddles. If that's what growing up is all about, count me out!"

My concerns about having to "give things up" turned out to be much like giving up mud puddles. Becoming a Christian meant giving things up that I wouldn't miss! Looking back, I can't believe I didn't eliminate those things earlier! Things like shading the truth, swearing, drinking and some other things that never really did me any good. So it wasn't a matter of giving things up. It was a matter of accepting better things!

Based on the mountain of evidence in the Bible that related to my own life, I decided that if the Bible had this much truth in it, there was a very good chance that it was all true. If God had 2,999 hits in a row, there's an extreme likelihood that His next at-bat would also result in a hit.

Then came the close. Jesus said, *"I am the way and the truth and the life. No one comes to the Father except through me."* (John 14:6) There's only one way to get to heaven . . . to accept this free gift, and I decided to do that.

I got down on my knees in a hotel room in Indianapolis, and I prayed . . . *"God, I confess that I have sinned, and I ask you to forgive me. I want You to come into my life and I want You to be in charge of my life, I want your principles to guide my life, and I want to follow you."* And at that moment, according to the principles in God's word, I was born again and I was a new creation in His eyes — I was a new creation! I had asked Him to be my Savior and Lord, to run my life, to be the Person who helps me make wise decisions instead of unwise.

But I haven't really gotten to the best part of the story! The best part relates to you, the person who's reading this book. The best part of this book hasn't really been written yet. The best part is what you're going to do with what I've just shared with you!

I want to challenge you right now, whether you're Atheist, Baptist, Catholic, Jewish, Methodist, Mormon, Muslim, Presbyterian, Seventh Day Adventist, Unitarian, or anything else! No matter what you claim to be, no matter what religion or denomination you were born into or what you've accepted to this date — I would like to challenge you to get a copy of the Bible and look into it and test it in your own life. If you're concerned about different versions, get copies of the original King James Version, the New International Version, and the New King James Version. You will find they each say the same thing when it comes to salvation and knowing God. You also have to figure if God is really as powerful as He claims, He can protect His Word and speak to you through it.

Test it and see if what I'm saying is true, and I believe you're going to find that it's true in your life just as it's true in mine. But I can only tell you about my life; I can't tell you about yours. I don't know what you're going through; I don't know the trials and difficulties that you have. However, I'm firmly convinced that God's Word, the Bible, does have answers for all the difficulties that we have while we're here on earth. And it explains a lot about what's going to happen when we leave this earth.

Some of the Bible's principles I haven't been able to prove because I haven't lived through them yet, but there have been so many which have been proven that I don't doubt the others.

Some people believe they're going to get a second chance, that they're going to be born into another lifetime. The Bible says, "... *man is destined to die once, and after that to face judgment.*" (Hebrews 9:27) Those people and the Bible can't both be right. God's word is so true in every other area of my life that I personally believe I'm going to die once and after that I'm going to face judgment. But, according to God's Word, according to God's Law, He has already forgiven me. He's already made provision for me to be in heaven and my future is eternally secure in heaven. I'm not going to be coming back here as another person, I'm not going to be reincarnated or anything like that.

Natural Selling Concepts

According to the Bible, I was saved when I accepted Jesus as my Lord and Savior.

So I want to suggest to you who are reading these words, if you have not accepted the claims that Christ has made about Himself in the Bible, at least get into the Bible and check it out. Some of the most fantastic stories I've ever heard are from people who have started reading the Bible just to see what was there and to see if they could prove that something wasn't true in their own life. Try it yourself, but be careful . . . Be ready for the God of the universe, the only living God, to reveal Himself to you!

I want to challenge you to challenge God to prove Himself. It is my belief that if you do this, you will not only find that it is all true. You will find that a decision to accept Jesus Christ as your Savior and Lord will be the best decision you could ever make. You will not only become your best as a person . . . you'll also be your best salesperson. I think you'll be your best family person, your best citizen — not just of the United States but of the world — and I think that God will be pleased with your effort. I pray that you'll do that.

There are groups of people all over the country who study the Bible and who are willing to help if you have any difficulties or questions about it or if you'd just like to learn a little bit more. If you would like to be put in touch with one of these groups, give me a call. My office number is (937) 291-0340. You can also contact me via e-mail at: info@B-Elite.com. If you'll give me a call or write, I'll be happy to try and help you personally, or put you in touch with someone who might be able to answer your questions and hopefully help to point you in the best direction.

Please do accept my challenge!

I can do everything in the sales process here except the

close. That's something that's between you and God. I'm just telling you what I know from my own life. I know that I had a need and that God gave me an Up-Front Contract early on. All through my searching I was presented with facts I could not refute. I had objections but God dealt with every one. And then, when it came my time to make the decision, I did go ahead and close. I accepted the gift of salvation from Jesus Christ and committed to follow Him as the Lord of my life. I hope and I pray that you'll do the same.

I want to wish you the very best in your life and your business, and I pray that as you go through your selling career you will find God, if you have not already, and that you will walk closely with Him.

God bless you.

About the Author

Carl Bromer is founder and president of Stellar Sales Training, Inc. In discussing his work philosophy, Carl speaks with sincerity and conviction: "My objective is to provide comprehensive, effective, real-world sales training . . . to teach sales principles and techniques that show business people how to succeed and have fun without compromising integrity or profitability."

The author's clientele includes manufacturers, distributors, consultants, thirty-year salespeople, entry-level salespeople and individuals selling virtually every kind of product and service.

Prior to his current career in sales training, Carl Bromer served as a technician at Kennedy Space Center on Apollo 4 through Apollo 12. He also served in the U.S. Air Force as an F-4 Phantom pilot; worked as National Sales Director for an international training company; and worked with Texas Instruments, Hamilton Avnet (billion dollar electronic component distributor) and Eskco (where he was responsible for sales, manufacturing and distribution).